T0354386

PREVIOUS BOOKS

Spiritual Wisdom for Peace on Earth From Sananda
Channeled through David J Adams

LOVE is the **KEY.** Part 1
Spiritual Wisdom from Germain
Channeled through David J Adams

LOVE is the KEY
Part 2

SPIRITUAL WISDOM FROM
GERMAIN
CHANNELED THROUGH
DAVID J ADAMS

DAVID J ADAMS

authorHOUSE®

AuthorHouse™
1663 Liberty Drive
Bloomington, IN 47403
www.authorhouse.com
Phone: 1 (800) 839-8640

Published by AuthorHouse 10/22/2018

ISBN: 978-1-5462-6551-1 (sc)
ISBN: 978-1-5462-6549-8 (hc)
ISBN: 978-1-5462-6550-4 (e)

Library of Congress Control Number: 2018909804

Front cover picture is the Marine Meditation Tapestry created by Kath Smith of Reynella in South Australia, the photograph of the Tapestry was also taken by Kath Smith.

Back cover Photo was taken on the camera of David J Adams, the T shirt was created by Tie Dye artist, Ruth Cary Cooper from USA.

Print information available on the last page.

DEDICATION

I Dedicate this book to my children, Nicky and Suzi, my grandchildren, Lauren, Matthew and Emily, and my great grandchildren, Ruby–Rae and Peyton, for they and others of the next generations will carry the Light forward and create the Peace that we all yearn for.

ABOUT THE AUTHOR

ADAMS, David John Patrick

Born: 28th April 1943

At: Mountain Ash, Glamorgan, South Wales, UK.

Moved to South Australia in 1971, Currently living in the southern suburbs of the city of Adelaide.

Began his Spiritual Journey as a result of the Harmonic Convergence in late 1987.

In 1991, he was asked by Beloved Master Germain to undertake a global Meditation based on, and working with, the Consciousness of the Oceans, which was called the Marine Meditation.

In 2009 he was asked to address a Peace Conference in Istanbul to speak of the Marine Meditation and his work for World Peace through meditation.

David J Adams

He is a Songwriter, a Musician, an Author and Channel, but most of all a **SERVANT OF PEACE**.

David began bringing through information from a variety of Masters and Cosmic Beings in the form of Meditations around 1991. It was not, however, until after the year 2000 that he began to channel messages in group situations and in individual sessions. Most of these messages were not recorded or transcribed so remain shared with only a few people, but in 2009 the messages being brought through in the weekly Pendragon Meditation group began to be recorded and transcribed by Kath Smith and sent out around the world on David's own Pendragon network.

David's special Guide and Mentor has been 'The Germain, the I am that I am', but he has also worked extensively with – and channeled - Sananda, Hilarion, Djwahl Khul, AA Michael, The Merlin, The Masters of Shambhala, as well as Arcturian Sound Master Tarak and his own Home Trinity Cosmic Brother Ar'Ak.

(Contact email – djpadams8@tpg.com.au)

ACKNOWLEDGEMENTS

I, David J Adams, would like to acknowledge three special Earth Angels.

Heather Niland/Shekina Shar - who helped me to awaken to my Journey in 1987 and connected me to my Beloved Friend "The Germain", she was a mentor, guide and teacher way ahead of her time.

Meredith Pope – who walked in the same shoes as me in those difficult early years as a fellow 'weekender' at The EarthMother Centre, and was - and still is - an inspiration to me.

Krista Sonnen – An Harmonic and Earthwalker, who helped to build the bridges to my Spiritual and Cosmic friends by persistently urging me to allow them to speak through me in private sessions, then in group sessions. Without her support these messages would not be here.

David J Adams

I would further like to acknowledge **Kath Smith** – A spiritual Being of immense Love and Joy who initiated the recording and transcribing of the messages received in Pendragon so that the messages from our 'other Dimensional friends' would not be lost forever. Also **Takara Shelor,** who combined her Global Water Dolphin Meditation with the Marine Meditation in 1998 and has organized the Marine Meditation website as an adjunct to her own Dolphin Empowerment website ever since. Also **Kaye Ogilvie**, Intuitive Spiritual Artist, who Painted all the Labyrinths walked during the Marine Meditations, as well as many other inspirational images that have assisted my Journey of Growth.

I also acknowledge all those here in Australia and those throughout the World who have supported me and encouraged me over the years, and in particular, **Barbara Wolf and Margaret Anderson**, who's vision and hard work has made this book possible.

BLESSINGS OF LOVE, JOY AND PEACE TO EACH AND EVERY ONE OF YOU.

DAVID J ADAMS

FOREWORD

"We don't know more, we don't know better, we just know Different"

This phrase, or variants of it, pops up from time to time in messages from most of our Spiritual and Cosmic friends, including Beloved Germain. What they are saying, of course, is that their messages are never intended to *'tell us what to do'*, they are simply providing a different viewpoint on life, on the Earth Planet and on your own journey towards Enlightenment, your own Ascension.

Three Key words appear constantly. They are *'Perception'*. *'Perspective'*, and *'Discernment'*.

'Perception' is how you understand things from your current level of Consciousness or awareness. *'Perspective'* is how the same scenario can be viewed from a different Dimensional Frequency, and *'Discernment'* is how you determine in your Heart

which viewpoint and which information is relevant to you at this particular time for your growth.

I hope you will embrace and consider the information provided through the messages in this book and then *'Discern'* what is right for you, for ultimately it is *Your Heart* that guides your Journey of Growth.

Blessings of Love and Peace

David J Adams

INTRODUCTION

When I was awakened to my Spiritual Journey by the Harmonic Convergence of August 1987 I was 'introduced' to Beloved Master Germain by Heather Niland, who had worked with him for quite some time. It was not, however, until January of 1991 that I received my first direct message from Germain, when he invited me to begin a Global Meditation based on the 'Consciousness of the Oceans of the World'. I have to admit that at first I thought it was a mistake and that the message was meant for Heather herself, until she smiled and said "David, don't you realize the message is for you?", as soon as she uttered those words, energy raced up and down my spine like electricity, and I realized she was right.

That began a wonderful partnership that has continued to this day. I ran the Marine Meditation for 22 years at 8pm (wherever you were in the World) on each Equinox, until my own Moana Beach based

Meditation came to an end at the September Equinox in 2012 after 44 Meditations had been held.

This was significant in that I have always worked with Beloved Germain in the vibration of the number 8, so 44 (8) meditations at 8pm on an 8 Beach, seemed appropriate. Interestingly, perhaps, Germain conducted the Meditations through me for the first 8 years from 1991, but was then joined by Masters Hilarion and Djwhal Khul for the remainder of the time.

The messages within this Book are but some of the many Messages of Love and Joy and Self Empowerment that Beloved Germain channeled through me within the Pendragon Meditation Circle. In the Messages he always referred to himself as 'The Germain' as if that were a title rather than a name, but to me, I guess he will always be Beloved Germain.

I hope his words of Wisdom resonate within your Hearts and give you upliftment on your Journey of Growth.

Blessings of Love, Peace and Joy.

David J Adams
(djpadams8@tpg.com.au)

CONTENTS

1

THE THREADS OF YOUR JOURNEY

(The Circle opens with the Sounds of the Tibetan Bowls and the Blessings Chimes)

Relax, become aware of your breathing. Draw into yourself the energy of Silver, feel yourself fill with the Divine Feminine energies. Feel yourself becoming empowered and aligned, melding together within yourself the Divine Masculine and the Divine Feminine, bringing yourself into a state of *ONENESS.*

Beloved Ones, I am The Germain, the I am that I am.

I come to you tonight to celebrate with you the energies of the Marine Meditation. As you are all aware, the purpose of holding this Meditation at a specific time wherever you are in the World, is to allow for this wave of energy to flow around the Planet. But when the energy flows around the Planet it does not come to a brick wall and stop at the end of 24 hours, it continues to flow around and around, embracing the Earth, embracing the Oceans endlessly.

Each time you come together for your Marine Meditation you empower that flow of energy – that flow of Love, that flow of Light - building strand upon strand a *Tapestry of Light and Love*.

The time has now come for each and every one of you to set aside the individuality of your Being, and to embrace *ALL THAT IS.*

On the evening of the Marine Meditation you spoke of the threads of your journey, drawing them into a Oneness in the beautiful quilted wall hanging that you now have (*See front cover*). It speaks of this most powerfully and most clearly as it brings together the threads of your Labyrinths, the threads of the *'Sounds'* of your Labyrinths, the *'Harmonic Notes'* of your Labyrinths, the *'Beings of Light'* that carried those harmonic notes, bringing them all into Visual Oneness within that quilted wall hanging.

Each time you gaze upon it you will be reminded of the need for you to begin to perceive your journey in its wholeness, not in its individual components.

You have isolated yourselves within your own journey for far too long, it is time to rise up with the *EAGLE* and look down upon your journey from a higher perspective, to bring together the threads of your journey into a fullness, into a *ONENESS*.

When you look upon your journey as isolated bits and pieces, you fail to understand the fullness of your journey. As you move forward over the next period of time into other Dimensional Frequencies, you need to look into the whole of your journey, you need to embrace the whole of your journey, for you are now *ONE* with *ALL THAT IS*, not only within this Earth Planet of yours, but within the whole of the Cosmos.

You are expanding energy bodies radiating powerful Light and powerful Love, connecting with others, becoming the Light of immense power – the Light of Divine Love and Divine Peace.

Allow your Hearts to guide you, allow your minds to follow, for together they will begin to understand that your journey is not segments, it is threads – threads of power, threads of Light, threads of Love, woven together – a ***Tapestry of Love***.

You will continue to work with the Marine Meditation, which does not simply happen twice a year, it happens and it creates a wave of energy that builds upon itself and weaves upon itself each time you come together, and with the assistance of the Oceans of your World these energies will continue to embrace the Planet with Love, with Light, with Peace and with Joy.

The Human journey is often one of peaks and troughs, but it is a continuous journey, not a fragmented journey. Each of you determined before you came into your physical vessel that you would move spiritually from point A to point B. a journey of determination.

Although within your physical vessel you have forgotten the intent of your journey, within your Heart you remember, and you persevere.

All your Spirit Friends are in awe and admiration of your tenacity, your determination to uplift yourself and uplift the Planet into the realms of Cosmic Light.

As you gaze upon your quilted wall hanging, be reminded to draw the threads of your life into **ONENESS**, to see all of your journey, to embrace the whole of your MULTIDIMENSIONAL SELF.

I look forward to joining with you again at your Marine Meditation, to embrace the Love within your Hearts, to share that Love with the Earth and with the Cosmos.

I Bless you, each and every one of you.

Feel the Silver within your Hearts begin to Sound its Melody of Light.

And so it is

(27th September 2010)

2

CREATE LIGHT AND LAUGHTER, AND MIRACLES WILL OCCUR ON YOUR PLANET

(The Circle opens with the Sounds of the Tibetan Bowls, the Blessings Chimes and the drum)

Greetings Beloveds. I am the Germain, the I am that I am.

We join you this evening to embrace the *Light of Love* within your Hearts, and to ask that you - and through you, that all other Light Workers and Way Showers on the Planet Earth - embrace at this time, the energies of *Beloved Dolphin - The energy of playfulness,*

> *The energy of joyfulness,*
> *The energy of upliftment, and*
> *The energy of community.*

As we sit and watch your Earth move into its period of transition and change, we perceive a mist of trepidation flowing across the surface of your world. As more and more humans awaken to the dramatic changes that are about to take place upon your Earth, the seeds of fear are the first to be shown – that inner trepidation - not knowing what is to come.

It is important at this time, that the mists of trepidation not be allowed to become the fog of fear.

As you well know, within a fog, Light is dissipated and diluted, and at this time, it is important for Light to shine on and through the Earth and all upon it.

It is so easy to move from trepidation into joyfulness, by perceiving the changes that are ahead as opportunities, opportunities to create your new Earth with the Magic in your Hearts, with the Love and the Light within your Hearts. To use your imagination to create what uplifts you, instead of that which enslaves you.

The energy of beloved Dolphin is the perfect antidote to trepidation and fear. As you focus upon the Dolphin, you are immediately struck by its playfulness, by its joyfulness, by its coming together in community - a community of Light and Laughter.

We ask you now to draw into your Being the energy of the Dolphin, to embrace the upliftment, the laughter within your soul.

Let us take a moment. Let us determine within our Hearts and our Minds, to dissipate this mist of trepidation, and replace it with the sunshine of Laughter, Joyfulness, Beauty.

The power to do this lies within your Hearts.

Take a moment now to imagine yourself as a Dolphin, leaping from the water, diving to the depths, playing with each other, feeling the Love, feeling the Laughter, feeling the Joyfulness.

As you do this, you begin to dissipate the mists of trepidation.

You begin to create the vibration of Light.

You bring the Sunshine into the world - the Sunshine of Love.

Feel yourself dancing within your Hearts. Feel the upliftment. Look out upon the Earth and project the Love, and the Light, and the Laughter.

It is so important to share your laughter, to not become steeped in the seriousness of change.

Create Light and Laughter, and Miracles will occur on your Planet.

Are you feeling the Dolphin energies flowing through your veins?, flowing through your auras?, feeling the joyfulness, rising up within every atom of your Being?, allowing your Light to break through the mist, to clear the areas of the Earth that remain in darkness?

Come together in community, in groups such as this, and reach out to each other with a smile on your face, with joy in your Heart and with a sense of utter delight.

With every change you perceive in your life, the possibilities are endless, but the possibilities of Joy and Laughter are the greatest gift you can give to the Earth at this time.

Feel yourself moving through the currents of life with ease and grace, for the joy that is ahead.

We urge each and every one of you to embrace the Laughter, and the Light, and the Love that you are all capable of creating from the depths of your Being.

We will be with you sharing our Light, our Love, and our Laughter.

Lift your spirits to the sky. Lift yourself into that state of bliss that comes from being truly happy within your Hearts.

Our blessings are with you.

(16th January 2012)

3

FEEL AND KNOW YOUR OWN BLESSEDNESS

(The Circle opens with the Sounds of the Tibetan bowls and the Blessings Chimes)

FEEL the sound of the Blessings Chimes, like raindrops in your Heart, filling you with a new Light and a new Love, raindrops sprinkling down to the very depth of your Being, and allowing new shoots of Light to grow and be empowered by the raindrops of Love.

It is important, Dear Hearts, to learn to *bless yourselves*. All too often you look out at your world and you send your blessings to others, to other Beings of Light, to other aspects of your Planet, but you rarely take the time to *bless yourselves*, and yet, Dear Hearts, blessing one's self is the most important aspect of your life, of your growth, of your acceptance of your Divine Beingness, for each of you are truly blessed by being on this Planet, at this time.

Yes it is true that there are times when you perhaps do not feel blessed at being here at this time, but you have **chosen** to be here, and that in itself is a blessing, for you know in your Soul Dimension that YOUR Light, YOUR Love, is ESSENTIAL to the Ascension of the Earth Planet itself, and to all life upon and within the Earth.

You are doing what you chose to do, and you have faced the challenges of many lifetimes on this Planet, and steadfastly you have returned to begin again, to contribute more and more of yourself to the Ascension of the Earth.

It is time to honour and accept the blessings you bring to the Earth at this time, and in so doing to FEEL the blessings within yourself.

Beloveds, I am The Germain - The I am that I am, *and I come tonight to ask you to FEEL and KNOW your own Blessedness.*

We have spoken to you often about our admiration of those of you who have chosen to be on the Earth

Planet at this time, and we have meant that most sincerely, for you are indeed all ***Blessed Beings of Light - courageous Beings of Light*** - although from time to time you hesitate and you wonder if you are doing enough, if you are being enough, and you forget to bless yourselves, and to feel the Love that ***WE*** have for you, that the Earth has for you.

But now, Dear Hearts, you have moved into the Dimension of Oneness, and you must feel, and be open to the blessedness of ALL that is.

It is understandable that each and every one of you goes through times of having doubts. That is part of your journey, but you know on a Soul level, you know you are in the right place, at the right time to ***BE*** who you are, and ***being who you are is the 'doing' that you sometimes do not perceive.***

You confuse activity with action, and simply being in your Love and being in your Light creates great action throughout the Earth, for each time you breathe, you breathe out your Love, and that breath vibrates through every part of the Earth, for you are ***ONE WITH ALL THE EARTH***.

So when you listen to the Sound of your Blessings Chimes, do not feel that it is purely for others, know that you are blessing yourselves. You are opening your Hearts and sharing the Love and the Light from deep within you.

So, listen to the raindrops in your Heart as the Blessings Chimes sounds with Love, *__of you, to you, and for you__*.

    Feel blessed

    Be blessed

    And allow your Heart to bless everything within the ONE.

(13th May 2013)

4

SOMETIMES THE 'NEED TO KNOW' DESTROYS THE FLOW

(The Circle opens with the Sounds of the Tibetan bowls and the Tingsha bells.)

Allow the resonance of the Sound to open and activate every Light particle within your Being, leaving behind the limitations of the past and embracing the wide expanses of the future, a future based in the Higher Realms of Light, and the Higher Sound resonances.

Allow and encourage yourself to feel Blessed within yourself, to feel Blessed for being in this place, at this time, a time of great change, but also a time of great opportunities, infinite possibilities, and YOU, through the wisdom in your Hearts, will create from these possibilities the New Earth of Love, of Peace, and of Harmony.

David J Adams

Greetings Dear Hearts, I am the Germain - The I am that I am.

I embrace each and every one of you with infinite Love, and I applaud your courage for having chosen to be here at this time, to assist the Earth and all upon the Earth, and within the Earth, to move into an *Ascended Reality of Light*.

It is easy to lose yourselves in the day to day rationale of your lives and to think that nothing is happening, but nothing could be further from the truth. The enormous explosion of Light that took place upon the Earth at the time of the recent Equinox has changed the course of the Earth's Ascension dramatically. *The intensity of that Light was so great it took the whole of the Cosmos by surprise.*

You could say, Dear Ones, there has been a mad scramble amongst your Spiritual friends and amongst your Cosmic friends to readjust *THEIR* visions of the future, as a result of this explosion of Light.

Those who you call the Masters have gathered together at Shambhala since that time to redeploy their energies, to reassess how best they / we can assist the Earth at this time.

Also, the Sound Masters of the Cosmos have gathered together at Arcturus, again to reassess how they can best assist the Ascended Earth, for as you well know, the Earth is held in balance by Sound, by Sound Vibrations, and the New Earth - being of a greater Light frequency - requires a different Sound frequency to hold it in balance, to hold it steady.

So, all the Sound Masters of the Cosmos were called together to work out what needed to be done - just as we in Shambhala were working out what needed to be done.

Rest assured, Dear Ones, we will support you and the New Earth with every fibre of our Beings, with all the Love in our Hearts, and with all the Peace and Harmony that it is possible to create.

YOU, through your desires, through the Light in your Hearts will create the fabric of the New Earth, and WE will sustain that fabric with our Light and with our Sound. We will work with the Crystalline Structure of the Earth Planet, and we will work with the Consciousness of the Oceans of the Planet, to enable the New Earth to sustain itself in the Higher Light Frequencies, and not allow it to fall back into the depths of duality once more. You have called for this, and we are helping you in every way possible.

You will feel and experience many changes in the times ahead, and we ask you to remain positive at all times, to look for the **Light** instead of the dark, to support the **Love** instead of the fear, *to follow your Hearts*.

You have lived many times upon this Planet, a Planet of duality, and you have lived consistently with the duality of cause and effect, but because you have existed more within your minds than within your Hearts, you have focused always too much on the 'cause' and not enough on the 'effect'.

Perhaps you may allow me to create a scenario for you to think of –

> *You are sitting in your lounge room and your child, or a loved one, or a good friend, comes bursting into the house, filled with excitement, filled with Joy, and you hug them, and you dance with them and you absorb their energies of excitement and joy, and then you let them go, and they dance from the house still excited - and you feel uplifted.*

LOVE is the KEY

Now let us look at the alternative scenario –

*Again you are sitting in your lounge room, and in rushes your child, your loved one, your good friend, filled with excitement, filled with Joy, and instead of embracing them, you sit them down, and you start asking them questions about what it is that has caused them to be so excited, so filled with Joy, and as you ask them and as they struggle to tell the story of what has created this within them, they begin to lose a little of that joyfulness, a little of that excitement, and when the story is completely laid before you, you cannot see what it was within the event that created such excitement for **them,** because **you** are not them, and when they leave, you are left feeling flat, and they also feel their Joy diminished.*

Which of these two scenarios are most familiar with you in this lifetime or in past lifetimes? I believe, if you are honest with yourself, you would say *"the second scenario is very familiar",* for you have been so obsessed with finding the 'cause' that you have forgotten to enjoy the 'effect'.

In the New Earth Frequencies you will let go of this need to know the 'cause', you will simply react and embrace the 'effect', you will embrace the Joy, you will embrace the excitement, and it will not matter to you what has caused this, all that will matter to you is that it exists – the upliftment, the excitement, the Joy, the Happiness. *It exists and it is being shared with you.*

You will no longer diminish THEIR enjoyment by questioning and judging the 'cause'. *You will, instead. simply embrace what is - the energies of Joy, of Love, of Upliftment.*

You see, Dear Ones, *sometimes the need to know destroys the flow.* Think about that for a moment. Think about those times in your lives when you could have, should have, simply embraced and shared the Joy and not worried about what created it in the first place. For what created it for that person would not necessarily create it within you, but does that matter? No, what matters is the sharing, what matters is the Joy itself, not the underlying cause.

I am not asking you, Dear Ones, to look back and judge yourself harshly, I simply ask you to look at how you have reacted in the past, and to know deep within your Hearts that one of the changes that is taking place within you now is an acceptance that what *IS*, is important, not how it came to be.

Sometimes you need to let go of the need to know, and simply allow the energies to flow. For when they flow freely they become a part of you, and you become a part of the flow itself and each of you feel uplifted by the other, not diminished, not limited in any way.

This, Dear Hearts, is the excitement of the New Earth. I ask you now to share that excitement with me, to share that joyfulness with me, but do not ask me why I am so excited, or so joyful. Simply embrace what I bring you tonight – the Joy the Excitement - and carry that in your Hearts as you move through the changes and take your rightful place amongst the stars.

I embrace you, and I bless you, and I share with you tonight my Joy and my Excitement over what is to come.

(12th November 2012)

5

LOOK AT YOUR LIFE
THROUGH YOUR HEART

(The Circle opens with the Sounds of the Tibetan Bowl and the Crystal Bowl.)

Allow the whole of your Being to be embraced by the Sound vibrations. Feel the upliftment within yourself that the vibrations of the bowls create within you.

Feel yourself becoming aware of every part of your physical Being. Feel yourself becoming aware of the bridge between your physical Being, and your Higher Self, and through your Higher Self, to all the multi dimensional aspects of yourself.

For even within your physical vessel you operate on many Dimensional levels, some of which you are aware, and some of which occur in your dream times, and fades from the consciousness of your mind as you awake - but remain constant deep within the Heart of yourself.

Greetings Beloveds, I am the Germain - The I am that I am.

The portal between the calendar years that you have on the Earth plane provides an opportunity for each and every one of you to reflect upon what has been on your journey in the past year.

It provides you also with the opportunity to let go of all judgements of what has happened on your journey, and to simply accept and give thanks for all that has occurred, whether you perceive those events as positive or negative, good or bad, they have all created who you are now, as you stand between the gateways of the year.

You are encouraged to look back, to let go of all those things that no longer serve the journey that you are on. *That is a discernment, Dear Ones, not a judgement,* for you are not saying that those aspects that you are letting go were less than positive on your journey. You are simply acknowledging they are no longer relevant to the journey ahead.

Once you have reflected, and given thanks for all that has been, it is time to turn and look at the year into which you are moving.

On your Planet, Dear Ones, you are encouraged to make New Year's resolutions, and yes it has become something of a joke amongst many, because New Year's resolutions are perceived only in the limitations of your physical Dimension, but it is indeed an opportunity to look at where you wish your journey to go.

It is a time to look beyond the limitations of your physical Dimension, to call upon your Higher Self, to look upon the pathway ahead. For you see, what you wish to create you have to focus upon, and that is what a resolution in reality is.

Let go of your perceptions of the limitations of resolutions about inconsequential things in your life, and focus instead on the highest spiritual aspects of your Being.

You are moving into a powerful year of 2012. In your minds many images have been created in regard to this particular time - the ending of cycles - the beginning of new cycles - the coming together that creates change, but your Planet is still one of free will. It is therefore for you to determine what your pathway ahead will be.

I come this evening to offer you two resolutions for the year to come, two simple resolutions – the first may be individual, but is also a collective Humanity resolution, and it is simply to *"look at your life through your Heart"*.

Construct that in your mind at this moment, and say to yourself *"I resolve to look at my life through my Heart"*.

The moment you begin to look at your life through your Heart, you will change your journey. You will see miracles occurring in your life, simply because you are working with the energy of Love, the energy of your Heart.

2012 is an important year of the Heart. Say to yourself now – *"I resolve to look at my life through my Heart"* - and feel its power!

The second resolution I offer to you tonight is an extension of the first resolution. It is quite simply - *"I resolve to create the pathway of my life through the Love and the Light in my Heart"*.

You cannot achieve the second resolution until you adopt the first resolution, but once you have begun to look at your life through your Heart, you will realise that you create your pathway - and the pathway for the whole of humanity - simply by working with the Love and the Light deep within your Heart.

You have spent eons of time working through your minds, and now it is the time of working through your Hearts. *It is through your Hearts that you will achieve the Enlightenment you seek, the Enlightenment we all seek.*

The Heart is the primary powerful energy of 2012, for the whole of Humanity.

Take a moment to repeat to yourself that second resolution – *"I resolve to create the pathway of my life through the Love and the Light within my Heart"* - and feel the power of that energy!

As I have said, Dear Ones, you are on a Planet of free will. I cannot command you to adopt these resolutions. I can only offer them from the Love deep within my Heart to assist you on your journey.

Before I leave, I will also make mention of the fact that 2012 is the year of the Dragon, and *this powerful*

Circle is Pendragon, so the energy of this Circle will be amplified many times by the Dragon energy of 2012, so it is of great importance that within this Circle you focus on ***Love,***

> you focus on ***Light,***

> you focus on ***Joy,*** and

> you focus on ***Peace and Harmony*** within yourselves - and through yourselves - within Humanity's Consciousness.

Dragon energy is a powerful, powerful energy. I am confident you will work with it well.

I embrace you with my Love, and bless you. **I am The Germain - The I am that I am.**

And so it is.

(2nd January 2012)

6

I RESOLVE TO BE LOVE IN EVERYTHING I SAY, AND EVERYTHING I DO

(The Circle opens with the Sounds of the Tibetan bowls and the Blessings Chimes.)

Allow the vibrations of the Bowls and the Blessings Chimes to lift you into your High Heart, your Soul Heart that you may once again look out across the Earth from the highest perspective, seeing the new energies of the Earth, feeling the new Dimensional Vibrations of the New Earth, and feel the energies of *BLISS* flowing through every particle of your Being, lifting you upwards in Light until you feel as if you are floating high above the Earth in Total Serenity, Total Harmony.

Feel the oneness with all that is. Look down upon the Earth and see the new Light frequencies radiating forth from the Heart of the Earth. Feel their power, feel your power, feel the oneness.

Greetings Dear Hearts, I am The Germain - The I am that I am.

You are not surprised at my visit tonight, for again it is that time of your year that you call your New Year's Eve, the time for looking back on the year that has passed, and remembering and embracing all the wondrous things that have happened in your life during that time, and also embracing those aspects of your life that have not been so wonderful - at least in your perspective of that time - for the year just passed has been one of monumental change for the Earth itself, but also for each and every one of you. Some of you have recognised the changes, and others have simply felt "unease", knowing that something is happening, yet not quite being able to put a finger on it. Do not worry, Dear Hearts, all will be revealed to your Hearts in the appropriate time.

At the beginning of 2012 I came to you and offered you a resolution - something that Humanity loves to have at this time of the year. I asked you *"to resolve to look at life through your Heart"*, and many of you have done so, and have seen the world in a totally different Light than you had before, and even seen yourselves in a different Light than you had before, for when you look at life through your Heart, you are not distracted by the chatter of your mind. You are simply seeing and feeling the vibrations of the Earth and of Humanity's Consciousness.

And, as your perspective has changed, your directions in life have begun to change. So I have come tonight to give you a resolution for the year to come, for 2013 - the beginning of your journey in the New Earth Frequencies. It needs to be a simple resolution, for this is not a time for complexities, it is a time for simplicity. So I come tonight and ask you *"to resolve, to BE LOVE in everything you say, and everything you do".*

Such a simple desire, such a simple intent, and yet one that has profound results for yourself and those around you if you adhere to your New Year's resolution.

So when you wake tomorrow morning on the first day of your New Year, say to yourself *"I resolve to BE LOVE in all I say, and all I do".*

Now you might say, "what does **"BE LOVE"** mean?" Dear Hearts, Humanity has diluted the meaning of the world 'Love', and tried to limit it to a special and specific relationship between two people, or perhaps a group of people - an expression of an emotional attachment. But as we have told you many times – Love is an energy - and it is an energy so powerful and so profound that Humanity has feared it for so long, they have 'chipped' away bit by bit, given different words to express different parts of the overall energy of Love, and reduced it to this limited form of interpersonal relationships.

And yet, in your Hearts, you know that Love is much greater than that, *Love is not something that you necessarily understand, it simply IS.* You know you have Love for members of your own family, and yet you do not have that Love relationship that you have with others. It is a knowing, it is an understanding of the power, the energy of connection, of Oneness.

It may surprise you to know, Dear Ones, that if you open a door for someone to go through, that is not a mere courtesy – it is an act of LOVE!. Why are you so afraid to admit to that within yourself? You are saying to this person, "I Love you", even when you do not know them, for you are simply opening your Hearts, and sharing that energy of Love.

You call these things courtesies, good manners, you have many other terms that you have separated in your Dimension of duality, when in reality all these things come together under the one umbrella - the umbrella of Love, the energy of Love - and when you say "thank you" to someone, you are again saying to them "I Love you".

Does that sound strange to your ears, Dear Ones? Does it send shivers down your spine, shivers of fear that you are daring to open yourself to let people know that you are a Being of Love, and that what you give to people is this incredible power of Love?

It is time to let go of the limitations, Dear Ones, they have no place in the New Earth, for the New Earth is about *LOVE, the complete, the total vibration and energy of Love,* so allow yourself to go into your Soul Heart and to speak from that Soul Heart and know that even in the incidental things that you appear to do, you are radiating outwards LOVE. *The words you speak to others need to be filled with that energy of LOVE. Your actions need to be filled with the energies of LOVE.*

That is what we mean when we say *"BE LOVE"*. Acknowledge, Dear Ones, that *YOU ARE LOVE* in every breath, in every word, in every action you take. *YOU ARE LOVE incarnate on the Earth.*

Last year you looked at the world through your Heart, and you began to see how Love can create understanding, can create compassion, can create openness, can create oneness. *You observed it.* that is what looking through your Heart means Dear Ones – observing, but now the time for sitting back and observing has been completed. The time now is to *BE THAT LOVE* that you were glimpsing as you looked through your Heart in 2012, for the New Earth requires a new dynamic, a new dynamic of communication between people, between people and the earth - *the DYNAMIC OF LOVE.*

So I ask you once again as you write down your resolutions for 2013, make number 1, and perhaps the only one -

"I RESOLVE TO BE LOVE IN EVERYTHING I SAY, AND EVERYTHING I DO".

Blessings be upon each and every one of you.

I LOVE YOU.

I LOVE YOU.

I LOVE YOU.

(31st December 2012)

7

TURMOIL, TURMOIL, TURMOIL

(The gathering opens with the Sounds of the Tibetan Bowl and the Drum)

Greetings, Dear Hearts, I am the Germain, The I am that I am.

Turmoil, Turmoil, Turmoil.

Most of you are looking around your Planet at this time and seeing only Turmoil, and you are concerned, some are even suggesting to you that at this particular time you need simply to go back to bed, pull the Duna over your head and wait it out, that this is a time of doing 'nothing'.

Dear Hearts, Turmoil always appears when changes are taking place. Think perhaps of putting water into a kettle and then putting that kettle onto a hot stove, in a short amount of time the water starts to bubble,

Turmoil occurs, and as this happens changes are taking place within the water, and when the heat is finally removed part of what was, has been dissipated as steam, and what remains is a different form of water. Dear Hearts, this is exactly what is happening upon the Earth at this time, new energies are coming in from the Cosmos, mingling with the energies that currently exist upon the Earth Planet and a reaction is taking place, heat and water, if you like, and things begin to bubble, and Turmoil is created.

So we can understand, Dear Hearts, why some are saying 'put the Duna over your head, and wait it out', but, Dear Hearts, if you do that, when you pull the Duna off your head what will you witness? What will the changed Earth be like? It will be like something YOU have had no control over, YOU have had no input into the changes, and this will cause even more Turmoil upon the Earth Planet.

What needs to happen now, Dear Hearts, is *"Focus"*. Look around you, see the Turmoil, do not let that disturb you, do not let that raise fears within you, *Know that this is change happening!* and *know that as Masters, as co-creators upon the Earth Planet, you can and should participate in the changes taking place.*

Nothing simply appears out of thin air, or if it does, Dear Heart, it has no substance, Change has to come from within. Within the Earth Planet itself, within each Being of Light upon the Earth Planet. So, Dear Hearts, if you wish to be a part of the new Earth then you need to start creating that new Earth within yourself, not hiding away from it, not saying "Ah, the world is changing, I don't want to know about this", but to move inside your Heart and begin to *Focus* your Heart, your mind, on the kind of world that you believe needs to emerge from the changes taking place.

Yes, Dear Hearts, you have the ability to participate in the changes themselves, but you need to do that by going within and by focusing on creating within your Heart the seeds of the New Earth, the New World, and then allowing that to grow, nurturing it, nurturing it, with the energies of *LOVE*, and then allowing it to shine forth from every pore of your Being out into the World, participating in the changes.

Dear Hearts, it is easy to simply say that you want Peace on Earth, but saying it doesn't create it, only action within yourself can create these changes. *If you want a World of Peace, a World of Love, a World of brotherhood, a World of Oneness, then you need to make that desire a focus within YOU. You need to create the Peace, the Love, the Oneness, within yourself, and then radiate it forth,* acknowledging that others will be doing the same, and that your energies and their energies will be drawn together, for *'like is attracted to like'*, and as each individual creates within themselves the seeds of Peace, of Love, of brotherhood, of Oneness, once they start to reach out with that energy, they will find companion energies coming together, creating a greater Peace, a greater Love, a greater Brotherhood, a greater Oneness.

You will have noticed, Dear Hearts, the changes taking place, the Turmoil taking place is not only on a Global Political level, or a Global Climatic level, it is happening around you, in your local neighborhood, in your Cities, in your Countries, and for many of you it is happening within you, *You are changing! You are in Turmoil within.* The new energies are bubbling away, creating those bubbles within you, releasing all the dark energies of the Old ways, the old rules, the rules that create power one over another. These are being gradually removed from within you. If you go to bed and put the Duna over your head and simply wait it out, you will create nothing! you will not even recognize yourselves, for the changes will still go on whether you are participating consciously or not. The releasing will still happen, but what you will be left with is a vacuum within yourself, and where there is a vacuum there is always darker energies seeking to fill it.

But you can avoid that. Dear Hearts, simply by consciously focusing on what you may call your dreams, your desires for a better World, for a better life for yourselves. We do not, in our place, call these things dreams, we call them *'Plans waiting to be manifested'.*

I could come here today, Dear Hearts, and tell you that the Turmoil is all Illusion, for we have said many times your life is an illusion, but *change*, Dear Hearts, change is real and constant, and your Cosmic Friends and your Spiritual friends, they come together from time to time and they draw into the Earth Planet, at the behest of Earth Mother – for we never presume to give energies to the Earth that are not requested - So at the bequest of Earth Mother we draw new energies into the Earth Planet to create change, and that creates the Turmoil, so, perceive your dreams as simply reality waiting to manifest.

This one *(David)* often quotes the title of that song by the one you call John Lennon, the song *"IMAGINE"*. Well 'imagine' is not 'dreaming', 'imagine' is seeing in the future what is within your Heart now, creating it, when you imagine something you create it, you don't simply dream about it, *so imagining is an 'active' process of creating*.

You are soon coming up to the time you call the Wesak, the coming together of the Buddha energies, the Christ energies, the coming together of the Masters at Shambhala, and this is a perfect time, a perfect time to open your Hearts, to walk inside your Hearts and to begin imagining Peace, imagining Love, imagining Brotherhood, imagining *ONENESS*, and with every beat of your Heart put energy into that imagining, so that you begin to create a new *you*, and a new *Earth*.

Earth Mother is crying out for you to imagine a Planet of *Love*, a Planet of *Peace*, a Planet of *Harmony*, a Planet of *Oneness*, and I say to you today, take away the Duna from your head, open yourselves, fill your Hearts with Love and radiate it forth. You are in the energy now of the Unicorn, Dear Hearts, the energy of *Oneness*, make full use of the energies of the *One* year, to begin again to create, and you begin to create by *"IMAGINING"*.

Dear Hearts, we are all with you, we are all supporting you, but as we cannot gift energies to the Earth that are not requested by Earth Mother, we cannot gift to you what is not asked for by you, so know that we are here and feel free to open your Hearts and call upon us to help you Imagine the perfection with which this Planet of yours began.

A perfection that WILL come again as you create it one Heart at a time.

Blessings. Dear Hearts.

(6ᵗʰ May 2017)

8

THE FIRE OF FREEDOM

(The circle opens with the Sound of the Tibetan Bowl, the Blessings Chimes and the drum)

Greetings, Dear Hearts, I am the Germain, the I am that I am

Focus on your breathing. Breathe in deeply and breathe out deeply in a very gentle, loving way. As you breathe, feel those vibrations of Love radiating forth from your body, and being drawn into your body.

Focus on the word – *PEACE*. Allow the vibration of that word to be carried by your breath into and out of your body, and your whole energetic Being.

As you have been told many times before, *Peace is an energy.*

Peace is not simply a cessation of war. *It is a deep, powerful and profound energy that has to come from within your own Heart.*

But to allow the Peace within your Heart to flow out into the world and create change within your world, you first need to embrace your own personal Freedom.

Freedom is the bedrock of Peace. For people who are not free, who are controlled by others, cannot create the Peace within themselves!

You will have noticed with the events taking place in the Middle East, that what the population in various Countries in that area are calling out for initially, is Freedom for themselves, *The Freedom to be FREE!*

As they begin to radiate this desire for Freedom out into the world, and begin to create the changes necessary for them to become free, they begin to sow the seeds of Peace.

Although at times it may not look on the surface as though Peace is the outcome, you need to remember that those who seek to control others do not give up their power lightly. But they cannot prevail against the intensity of the desire within each individual in that area for Freedom.

It is not simply within these areas who are dominated by tyrants or by Military Juntas. It is not merely them, *ALL* Governments, even so called Democratic Governments exercise control over their people.

Many of these Countries will begin to see an upsurge within their populations of this desire for individual Freedom, and through that Freedom will emerge a Peace upon this Planet that we have hitherto never dared to dream of – much less achieve – over eons of time that Humanity has been in this place.

So, Focus your energies now on *The Fire of Freedom within yourself.*

-Freedom to choose
-Freedom to *BE*
-Freedom to Love
-Freedom to connect.

Peace will emerge when people are Free within themselves.

Freedom is the Light that moves away the darkness of fear and control – Freedom of Spirit, Freedom of Heart.

Breathe in the energy of Freedom
Radiate forth the energy of Freedom
As you allow the Light within you to shine, you are
Beacons for Freedom.

Freedom aligned with the energy of **LOVE**, creates *respect one for another.*

It moves away from the need to control and dominate others.

It accords *respect.*

It allows **Dignity.**

It embraces *ALL THAT IS.*

As you breathe in and breathe out, focus on the energy of Freedom, for freedom is within your Heart and within your Mind.

Freedom will create the Peace that the bulk of Humanity has yearned for, for so long.

Let the Sound vibrations carry forth your Light of Peace out into the world, out into the Cosmos.

David J Adams

We are Free!

Free at last!

Free at last!

Free at last!

PEACE WILL PREVAIL!

And so it is.

(28ᵗʰ February 2011)

9

UPLIFTMENT, UPLIFTMENT, UPLIFTMENT

(The Circle opens with the Sounds of the Tibetan Bowls and the Blessings Chimes)

Allow yourselves to relax totally, to move your Consciousness deep within your Heart, to allow your minds to *STILL*, and merge with the Love and the Light in your Heart.

Greetings Beloveds. I am the Germain - The I am that I am.

Your world is going through tumultuous times, but this should come as no surprise to all of you, for you have been awakened to these changes for quite some time. There should be no surprises to you, other than the content of the changes as they emerge, for you are prepared for the energies of change.

It is the energies of change that you need to focus upon - not on the outcomes of those energies as they swirl around your Planet, for these are many and varied - some you see - some you do not.

Changes are taking place at every level of life, deep within the Earth itself, deep within the Hearts of all those upon your Earth and within your Earth.

You are becoming increasingly aware that you are not alone upon this Earth as an intelligent Consciousness. Many other Beings of Light that have taken other forms are now beginning to speak to you, to converse with you. Your role is simply to open, and allow these communications to resonate deep within your Hearts.

You do not need to understand language - you simply need to embrace energies – energies of Light - and to allow those energies to uplift you.

When you find that energies are around you that do not uplift you – let those energies go their own way. Do not create judgments around these energies, simply because they do not resonate with your Heart. They may well resonate with someone else's Heart.

For each of you has a unique and individual resonance. Sometimes that is compatible with others, sometimes it is not. This is not judgemental – it is simply factual.

All energy upon your Earth and within your Earth has purpose. It has relevance to some aspect of the Light that continues to emerge and strengthen within and around the Earth.

The energy in the form of Sound is often misunderstood. *Harmony and disharmony are words of judgment.* Sound resonates – again, what resonates with one may not resonate with another. It is the same sound, so it is not harmonic and harmonious or disharmonious – it simply *IS*, until it connects with you. Then it becomes a choice – do you accept this energy as an upliftment in your life? Or do you allow this energy to go its way because it has no upliftment to you?

These are always the choices you are faced with in every moment of every day of your lives.

Focus totally at this time on feelings of upliftment within yourself. For this time of change is about uplifting the Earth and all upon the Earth.

Do not hold on to energies that do not uplift you.

Do not hold on to circumstances in your lives that do not uplift you.

As you move quickly towards the transformation of your Being, and the transformation of the Earth, you cannot hold on to energies that do not uplift you. For energies that do not uplift you are anchors, and you need, at this time, to flow freely with the energies of change.

Focus now, deep within your Hearts. Let go of all those energies that are not uplifting, that you have been holding onto from your past.

Feel the Love Energy resonate deep within your Heart, creating a pool of Serenity, and allow yourself to flow with this **Energy of Serenity**. Allow it to create within your lives the upliftment that is necessary for this next stage of your journey.

Take time to meditate. Take time to relax, for the times ahead are turbulent indeed.

Much on your Planet needs to change.
Be the observer.

Do not take on board energies that are less than the Light that you are.

Focus on the Sound of Love within your Being.

I leave you tonight with the word vibration that is the key in this time of transformation:–

UPLIFTMENT – UPLIFTMENT – UPLIFTMENT.

Embrace that vibration in your heart. Make it the key for your life at this time.

I am the Germain – The I am that I am.

(25th July 2011)

10

THE 'AWAKENING' WILL BE
REAL AND DYNAMIC

(The Circle opens with the Sounds of the Tibetan Bowls and the Blessings Chimes)

Focus your attention on the ever changing colours and the flickering lights upon the table at the centre of your Circle, and allow those colours to flow deep into your Being, creating a Rainbow Light deep within your Hearts. Each colour has its own frequency of Light and as they come together in **ONENESS** they create changes of vibrational frequency within you. Allow that to happen now, feel yourself begin to expand as the colour vibrations flow through you and meld into a Oneness at the centre of your Being, and feel yourself being lifted into new Higher Dimensional Frequencies. *Embrace each other, create a Oneness in the New Earth*

Dimensional Frequencies, for TOGETHER you create the power of ONE.

Greetings, Dear Hearts, I am the Germain - The I am that I am.

I have not been with you since the time of the Solstice when the Earth opened its Heart and cast forth the *Magenta Light of Peace and Love,* so it feels very special for me at this moment to be in the embrace of that Magenta Light, and to feel and see within that Magenta Light all the other colour vibrational frequencies that beloved Earth Mother is gifting to you, and to others out in the Cosmos.

For this is a time of great expansion of the Earth Planet within the Cosmos, finally the Earth is giving forth its true Light and being seen by all those within the Cosmos as a *'True Light Being'*, and beloved Earth Mother will continue to let the Magenta energies from deep within its Heart flow out across the surface of the Earth and out into the Cosmos, and more and more of Humanity will be awakened to their true purpose for being on the Earth at this particular time in the Earth's history. For it is indeed a time of monumental change, the veils that have hidden the true worth of the Earth have been cast aside and it shines brightly now in the Cosmos, and in so doing it attracts 'like' energies.

You have already been told this evening to expect a major influx of electromagnetic energies in the period to come, this has resulted from the fact that Mother Earth has shone brightly now her Magenta Heart and has called to herself the new Light frequencies that are required to ensure the future of the New Magenta Earth in a new majestic vibrational frequency.

Your spiritual friends are all in awe of the step that you have now taken on your Planet, you have closed the book on the darkness of the past and you have opened a new book, a book of empty pages waiting for the Love within your Hearts to write the future of the New Earth, and it is indeed from the Heart that the future of the New Earth will come. The electromagnetic energies that are flowing toward your Planet at this time are specifically designed to connect your minds to your Hearts - not in a subservient way, but in a unity way - so that your 'computer like brains' can truly be utilised for the benefit of the visions within your Hearts.

Think on that a moment, Dear Hearts, imagine that a moment - *utilising for the first time the full majesty of your brains to pursue the desires and dreams of your Heart.* It is like getting into a hot air balloon and letting go of the ropes and feeling yourself lift upwards, feeling yourself moving higher and higher, and your perspective of your Planet completely changes, and the Love deep within your Heart wells up and spills over and you know it is time to begin to create a new Earth model, and instead of coming up with problems, your minds - empowered by your Heart - will come up with 'solutions' to the many problems of the past.

The 'awakening' will be real and dynamic. Your spiritual friends also are beginning new journeys with empty pages to fill and we have all been called together once more at beloved Shambhala to see how we can assist you and the Earth Planet to absorb these new electromagnetic energies.

Have you been feeling underlying joyfulness within your physical bodies since the time of the Solstice? those moments when for no apparent reason you feel joyful, uplifted? This is the Magenta energy at work within you, Dear Hearts, and when this Magenta energy is empowered and integrated with the electromagnetic energies from Source, *imagine the possibilities!*

Focus your dreams, Dear Hearts, focus your desires, always in a way that encompasses *ALL*. This is not the time for self-centredness, although it is the time for self-awareness and self-acceptance, embracing the knowledge that you, as an individual, are part of the whole and can influence the whole. You are like one of those colours on your table coming together with all the other colours and creating a wonderful *Rainbow Ball of Light within your Heart*, and shining that Light forth for *ALL* to see, for *ALL* to feel, for *ALL* to connect with.

The coming together of this Circle creates a magnificent energy, imagine how more magnificent it will be when many, many more join together in 'ONENESS'. Yes, Dear Hearts, we have spoken to you many times about the 'Oneness' and your minds have always had difficulty understanding what that 'Oneness' is, but your Hearts, your Hearts have always known, and now with the Magenta energy and the electromagnetic energies coming together, your mind will be educated by your Heart, and you will know *Fully,* without any shadow of doubt, that you are *All One*, not just *All* upon the Earth, but *All* throughout the Cosmos, you are *All One*, and when you accept and acknowledge that, feel the power of it within you, for you are not separate, you are not alone, you are all a part of the *One Heart*.

<u>*YOU ARE LOVE, YOU ARE PEACE, YOU ARE JOY.*</u>

(24TH August 2015)

11

LOVE is the KEY

(The Gathering opens with the Sounds of the Tibetan Bowl, the Drum and the Peace and Harmony Chimes)

Greetings, Dear Hearts, I am the Germain, the I am that I am.

If you're looking at a world filled with darkness,
Then there's something you've forgotten to do,
You've forgotten to turn on the switch in your Heart
That allows your LOVE to shine through.
Walk your path in the Light of the LOVE in your Heart,
Be a Beacon for everyone to see,
Show the way, share your Light, and everybody in sight
Will realize that LOVE is the KEY.

Hahaha (chuckle), yes, Dear Hearts, I am quoting the words of a song that was gifted through this one *(David)* some ten of your Earth years ago, and I use the word gifted because, of course, it was indeed a message channeled from the Masters of Shambhala, just as this is a channel, the song was a channel.

You see, Dear Hearts, your Spiritual friends, the Masters of Shambhala included, use a whole variety of means to impart their messages to you and through you to Humanity, it may be a song, it may be a poem, it may be a prose, it may be 'Conscious writing', or it may just be that momentary flash of inspiration that suddenly comes into your mind, you know not from where, but it brings you that *"AHA"* moment in your life. And it is important, Dear Hearts, to share that knowledge, that wisdom, that message to as many people as you can, for sometimes it takes but a single word to open the door or unlock something deep within a Soul and begin the awakening process within that individual. It does not need to be a message such as this one, as I say it could just be a word or a line in a song that suddenly begins your awakening.

Dear Hearts, I bring you a reminder of this message today because many of you are looking around the World at this time and seeing only darkness, seeing only chaos, seeing only catastrophes, seeing conflict, pain and hurt, natural as well as man made catastrophes, and even though many of you at times try to withdraw yourself from this reality of your Planet, perhaps not looking at the news, or reading newspapers, you cannot hide from the energy, Dear Hearts, the energy of all these things are part of the Global Consciousness, and they Will permeate your Being, and they will create changes within your Being, they will *Dim your Light*, so to speak, *Unless,* unless you Consciously accept that this is happening and unless you Consciously reach within your Heart and click on that switch that opens your Heart and floods you, and through you, floods your environment with the *Deep Divine Love* that exists within each and every one of you.

It needs to be, Dear Hearts, a daily Conscious action by *You*. You do not avoid the energies that are swirling around your World, but you can be the beacon of Light within those energies if you so choose. If you choose to be *Joyful*, filled with *Love,* you will contribute in a positive way to the Consciousness of the Earth Planet, but if you hide away, then you contribute negatively to the Consciousness of the

Planet. ***There IS nowhere to hide, Dear Hearts,*** and even when you feel or perceive that you are doing 'nothing', you are always doing 'something', and that 'something', Dear Hearts, is radiating forth ***Your Light***, sending out into the World what is within ***You.***

We have told you many time, Dear Hearts, that you are existing on a Planet of 'Free will' for a purpose, for the learning purpose, learning how to discern, learning how to act, so you have the free will, you have the ***choice*** of how you create and conduct your own energy, so even when you are sitting around thinking you are doing nothing, you are still radiating your energies and contributing your energies to the Consciousness of the Earth Planet, and you need to decide what energies you contribute, do you contribute those energies that you accumulate from the Consciousness of the Earth Planet, these dark, chaotic energies that swirl around your Planet at any given time? or do you contribute the Love and the Light that you know exist deep within? do you ***Become the Beacon of Light?***

Think about that deeply, ***<u>WILL YOU BE THE LIGHT YOU CAME HERE TO BE?</u>*** or will you simply be a receptacle for the energies that flow around you, swirl around you, the darkness, as well as the Light? Oh yes, Dear Hearts, there are lots and lots of Beings upon the Earth Planet who have made the determination to *Be Their Light,* and daily they put out into the World the Love and the Light within them, and that too swirls around, and you are impacted by that, but is it enough to simply be absorbing *Their Light? when you could be contributing Your Light.* It does not need to be for a specific purpose, you do not look at perhaps one particular catastrophe upon your Planet and radiate your Light to that event, no, Dear Hearts, it needs to be holistic, simply radiating the *Love* and the *Light* out from your *Being* and contributing it selflessly, unconditionally, to the betterment of the Consciousness of the whole of the Earth.

So when you awaken, Dear Hearts, each day, let your first action be to reach within your Heart and flick that switch that allows your *Love* to shine through, not just for a moment, but for the whole of your day, you see, Dear Hearts, the energy of *Love* within you has no bounds, it is not a limited supply contained within your physical vessel, you are Multidimensional Beings, your *Love is Infinite, Your Light is Infinite,* but it is within your control, and you, only you, can choose to radiate forth that Love, that Light, to **Be the Beacon,** To stand tall in your knowing that you are a Being of Light, a Being of Love, and that you are here upon the Earth Planet at this time to **Make a positive difference to the Consciousness of the Earth.**

So, Dear Hearts, that is why I have come to remind you of that message from the Masters of Shambhala, the song that **"LOVE is the KEY",** so I will finish today with the second part of that message from the Masters, for just as it was relevant ten of your Earth Years ago it is relevant now, you see, Dear Hearts, in the Spirit realms there is no Linear time, everything is in the **'NOW',** and when you receive a message today, it is not just for this moment, it is for ever. You may have wondered why at times we refer you back to a message that was passed through you many years ago, it is because it is still relevant to the **'NOW'** Dear Hearts, so I invite you to share once more this powerful message that **"LOVE is the KEY".**

If you feel the world is crumbling around you,
And you can't work out just what you ought to do,
Reach into your Heart and turn up the flame,
And allow your LOVE to shine through.

David J Adams

Walk your path in the Light of the LOVE in your Heart
Be a Beacon for everyone to see,
Show the way, share your Light, and everybody in sight,
Will realize that LOVE is the KEY.

Dear Hearts, we are with you at all times, through thick and thin, through storms, through serenity, ***WE ARE ALL ONE, ONE SPIRIT, ONE LOVE, ONE LIGHT***. We Bless you and Love you.

(Note: an audio of the song, "LOVE is the KEY", can be heard and downloaded free of charge at ... https://soundcloud.com/david-j-adams/love-is-the-key)

(23rd October 2017)

12

I THANK YOU FOR BEING WHO YOU ARE, AND FOR BEING WHO YOU WILL BE!!!

(The circle opens with the Sounds of the Tibetan Bowls, the Blessings Chimes, the Rain stick and the Tingsha bell and the rattle)

Feel the silence within your Hearts pulse and beat out into the World, riding the waves of Sound, but sharing the realm of Peace. Reaching out to the stillness in the Hearts of every Being, and uniting in *Oneness* and a feeling of Deep Serenity. Embrace that Serenity, Now, through every pore of your Being. Allow yourself to be rocked gently in the arms of *Serenity*.

Greetings Dear Hearts, I am the Germain, the I am that I am.

I know, Dear Hearts, that my presence was expected this evening, for we have gathered together many times at this juncture of the Equinox, to work together, to play together, to be in Love together, to be enlightened by each other, and to be embraced by the *Serenity of the Creator*.

In the past, Dear Hearts, I have asked you to work with me through the Oceans of the World, and through the Beings of Light within those Oceans to assist in the upliftment of the Earth and the upliftment of Humanity, and that work has never ceased, even though we no longer meet in the way we did, the work and the Joy of that work has never ceased. It has simply changed form. For change, Dear Hearts, is constant, and what was relevant in your time scale 5 years ago, 10 years ago, is no longer relevant, it has moved on, it has expanded, it has become enlightened. But in *Oneness* we continue along the pathway of growth - individual growth, collective growth, and Planetary growth.

I can feel the energy within this circle tonight, the anticipation of the events that are about to occur. The new *Song of the Earth*, is already beginning to permeate through every fibre of your Being, you can sense it, Dear Hearts, you can feel it, you can practically *Taste it!* and it is a feeling of such **_ECSTASY._** All of us, throughout the Cosmos are feeling the same thing. We are filled with a New Joy, a New excitement, as the Beloved Earth Planet *Breathes* more powerfully than ever before, Radiates Light more powerfully than ever before.

Feel the Serenity within you, allow that Serenity to paint the Earth, giving it new Light, giving it new Glitter, for that is what the *Song of the Earth* will do, Dear Hearts, it will enable the Earth Planet to expand, and to Glitter amongst the Stars, proclaiming to all that it is now in its rightful place in the Universe, it has *Ascended into Light,* and all those upon the Earth have also *Ascended into Light.*

We have worked together long and hard, that work will not come to a close, it will simply change yet again as we strive for the Perfection of the Earth, and the Perfection of all upon the Earth, as you move closer and closer to the Heart of the Creator, the Vibrational frequency of the Creator, and you too will Glitter, just as the Lights on your Table Glitter and shine forth their many colours, pulsing, radiating, each one of you will *BE* as these Lights, Dear Hearts, and the whole of the Earth will be uplifted.

At our last gathering you were invited to come to Shambhala and spend some time with us, and I invite you again this evening to do the same, for when the *Song of the Earth* resonates and accumulates deep within the Earth, and the outer skin of duality and darkness is shed, You will be permanently in the Light of the Shambhala along with us.

I ask you once more to focus your Hearts on the Oceans of the Earth Planet, to communicate, to speak, to embrace, all the Beings of Light within the Ocean. Sing together with them, and with us, this *New Symphony of Love,* and feel your own skin of duality and darkness shedding away, as the essence of Serenity, and the essence of Ecstasy begins to throb deep within your Hearts, for this Serenity, this Ecstasy, will show, it will be the Glitter that others will see, and gradually begin to understand. For Serenity does not create fear, it creates *Love – Divine Love.*

Dear Hearts, *I THANK YOU FOR BEING WHO YOU ARE, AND FOR BEING WHO YOU WILL BE!!!*

(22nd September 2017)

13

BEGIN TO CREATE DESIRES WHICH ARE FOR THE HIGHEST GOOD

(The Circle opens with the Sounds of the Tibetan Bowls and the Blessings Chimes and the Drum)

Embrace the energy of Divine Love, allow it to fill every aspect of your Being, uplifting you, integrating you into the Oneness of all that is.

Greetings Dear Hearts, I am The Germain - The I am that I am.

You have been told on innumerable occasions that you are now in a Dimensional frequency where you are able to manifest your desires with ease and grace, and we have asked you to be most careful about the thoughts that you allow into your minds, because thoughts are the beginning of realities, and you will begin to manifest the thoughts and desires within yourself.

We are often amused when we speak to Humanity of manifesting their desires, that more often than not they begin to focus very narrowly on desires of the third dimension, desires perhaps of abundance, desires of meeting special people in their lives, desires that are of the past. But in this time of Oneness, in this Dimension of Oneness, we ask you to let go of those desires and to move instead into looking at the World, to looking at the wholeness of things, and to begin to *create desires which are for the highest good, and not simply for the personal good*.

It is time to reflect, Dear Hearts. upon what you can create for others, what you can create for Humanity as a whole.

You should therefore begin to think of what is needed in the World at this time, and how you as an individual can contribute your energies to creating what is needed, rather than what is personally or individually desired. Perhaps I might express it as *'need, not greed'*.

Do not necessarily look for expansion of yourself, for yourself, but look to express yourself for Humanity, for the Earth, for the *Oneness of all that IS*. Release the individuality which is part of the separation where you perceive manifesting as being solely about you.

The new Earth frequencies are about the *One*, not the *You*. Do you understand what I am saying Dear Hearts? Allow your minds to broaden their perspective, to look at the Earth, to look at the 'Whole of Humanity' and to begin the process of manifesting for everyone.

This process begins when you move from the isolation of your mind, into the Oneness of your Heart, and begin to create your dreams, your desires, and your expectations from within that Oneness of your Heart, not the isolation and separation of your mind.

So focus, Dear Hearts, deep, deep within your Hearts, and ask yourselves "what can I create and manifest for the highest good of all?", and your Heart will begin to create wondrous, magical things, and *your energy of Love will be the oxygen that makes those dreams and desires breathe themselves into reality.*

Think, feel and *BE* all this within the *Oneness of Love,* and you will begin to create a world of Peace, and Harmony, and Joy for *ALL.*

(22nd July 2013)

14

PERCEPTION IS EVERYTHING

(The Circle opens with the Sounds of the Tibetan Bowls and the Blessings Chimes)

Greetings Beloveds, I am The Germain – The I am that I am.

In this time of Earth Transition, *perception is everything*. Humanity has a long record of creating fear – within themselves, and within each other.

The easiest way to create fear has always been looking at the 'unknown'. The unknown has always been a source of great fear for Humanity. That is merely a perception. It is a perception that needs to change at this time of Transition.

Yes, indeed, there is great unknown in this Transition and this Ascension of the Earth Planet. For such an Ascension has never taken place in the Universe before, a time when the whole Planetary system, and all upon her ascends at the same time. Even we, in the higher realms, do now know with great certainty how everything is going to eventuate.

We do not look upon the unknown as a source of fear, we look upon the unknown as a source of great excitement. I am here tonight to invite each and every one of you to take a similar perception of the future, to look ahead at the great unknown with a sense of great excitement.

There will be many who will choose fear as their perception, but as the changes manifest and reality becomes apparent, the illusion of those fears will soon fade, for the Light of Love will banish the shadows.

As you look forward in your journey to the great unknown ahead, know within your Heart that the great unknown is filled with Light and Love, not filled with darkness any more. The darkness is behind you. The Light is ahead of you. The reason for this is quite simple Dear Hearts, *YOU are the LIGHT. And as you project your Light forward, shadows disappear, for you leave the darkness behind and walk into your own Light.* You create

a world of Light, a world of Divine Love, and there
can be no fear of that! How can you fear Love? How
can you fear Light?

So it is important at this time of Transition that you
hold steadfast within your Hearts to the Light and
the Love that you have taken great pains to create
in this lifetime, that you are now radiating forth out
into the World, sharing with others, allowing them
to see *Your* Light, allowing them to see how *Your*
Light lights up the journey ahead. Sharing with them
the wisdom and the knowledge that *They too* have
Light within themselves, Light within their Hearts,
and that *They too* can radiate that Light in front of
them to banish the shadows of fear, to embrace the
excitement of a new journey.

We, your friends in other Realms, are filled with
Joyous excitement. We ask that you too be filled
with this Joyous excitement. Changes that take place
on your Planet may not, on the surface, seem to
be of great benefit. Even now, at this time, when
you in this Country are seeing water covering great
parts of your land, you can choose to see this as a
tragedy, or to perceive it as a great cleansing. *Water
is a conductor of energy, do not forget. Send your
Light, your energy, to all those areas, and allow*

the water to carry your energy, your great Light, your great Love.

You can choose to look at the devastation, or you can choose to look at the courage, at the Light, at the Love, at the Compassion that these events are creating within Humanity.

I need only point your attention to the lines and lines of people coming to help those less fortunate than themselves – people who, in lesser times, would have ignored each other. So even within the apparent tragedy of flooding there is a great awakening within the Heart, and this is a cause of great excitement.

Yes, Dear Ones, we in other Realms would wish that it was not necessary for the Earth to shed its tears in this way, to release all that it has stored of the darkness. You can not be a part of the Earth Planet without accepting the need of the Earth to release its darkness also.

Beloved Gaia embraces you with great Love, and through her pain, and through her release, she reaches out to Light your Hearts with Compassion, with Love, with Gratitude.

Perception is everything, Dear Ones. I ask you now to perceive these events, to perceive the future of your Planet as exciting, as enlightening, as awakening.

We have spoken to you in previous times about the need to come together in Community, to come together in groups, and that is **Precisely** what is happening!!

In the face of perceived tragedy, the Hearts of Humanity are awakening once more. Communities are re-discovering their identity, their reality. They are letting go, letting go of old ways, and coming together once again in **Love**.

PERCEPTION IS EVERYTHING.

I AM THE Germain, The I am that I am.

My Blessings upon you

(19th January 2011)

15

YOU NO LONGER FEEL THE WIND, FOR YOU ARE THE WIND

(The Circle opens with the Sounds of the Tibetan bowls and the Crystal bowls.)

Let your Hearts dance to the rhythm of the Bowls, feeling yourself empowered and uplifted by the vibrations of Sound that call to your Heart, that call to your Soul, inviting you to open yourself fully to the new vibrations of the Earth, and the new relationship between the New Earth and the Cosmos, for this is no longer a separate dance of Love that the Earth is enjoying, it is now in Oneness with the Cosmic flow of Life.

The Earth itself is beginning to radiate its true Light within the Cosmos, connecting and reconnecting with energies of wisdom that have been waiting to enter the Consciousness of the Earth, and *ALL* upon the Earth, for we are all now in a state of *Oneness*.

We realise, Dear Hearts, that many of you are confused, you are so accustomed to the Dimension of duality and separation that it is difficult to embrace the energies of Oneness, because you no longer can feel them as separate from yourself, and it is a totally new experience to be *'within'* the energies of *All that is*.

You are accustomed to acknowledging energy as it relates to your own, but everything is now *ONE*. There is no conflict of energies, so how do you sense energies anymore? How do you recognise the differences between energies when there is no difference between energies?

Sit within your Hearts, open yourself and *feel* the Oneness, *feel* the lack of resistance. This is not something to be feared, Dear Hearts, it is something to be embraced. The absence of resistance in energy is the proof you have asked for when told you are moving into the Dimension of Oneness. It requires of you a totally new way of relating to everything and everyone around you. It requires you to speak and communicate through your Heart, for your Heart understands Oneness, when your mind does not.

If you continue to struggle in your minds to comprehend the differences, you will simply be holding yourself back from enjoying the totality of the shift that has taken place.

Let go of your need for resistance. Let go of your need for differences. Embrace what your Heart already knows – the true Oneness of all that is, and as you embrace that new Oneness, you will feel empowered, you will feel joyful to the point of being Blissful, for you no longer feel the wind in your face, for you are part of the wind.

Think about that for a moment, *You no longer feel the wind, for you are the wind.* You are energy - you have known this for some considerable time - you are energy, and now you are *'ONE'*_energy.

The only resistance, Dear Ones, is within your mind, so move from your mind into your Heart and *feel*, and *know* from deep within yourself that this *is* the new beginning. *You have become the wind, you have become the rhythm of the Sound, you have become the vibration of Love.* Do these words not uplift you, Dear Ones? do they not empower you, knowing you are *One* with the wind?

It is all about choice - *you choose to fight, you choose to resist, or you choose to LOVE, and you choose to BE*. Magical, seemingly miraculous things will happen in your life the moment you become the wind.

Are you thinking of that now? are you feeling yourself as part of the wind Dear Hearts? *Feel yourself not only part of the winds of the Earth, but the winds of the Cosmos, for there is no difference between the two anymore. All is one.*

When we speak now of energies flowing in from the Cosmos, you will not feel these energies, for you *are already* these energies. They are a part of your own expanded Being, your Multidimensional Being - no resistance, part of the flow.

So many times we have spoken to you about this, about being a part of the flow, well now Dear Hearts, in the Dimension of Oneness, you are a part of the flow, and because you are part of the flow, you no longer *'feel'* the flow.

Your Heart understands this Dear Ones, but it may confuse your mind, for *if your mind does not feel the wind, it believes there is no wind.*

So let your Heart speak to your mind and tell your mind *'You are the wind, you are one with all that is'.*

Dear Hearts, I am the Germain - The I am that I am - but I am not - for

I am ONE with each and every one of you.

I am a part of you.

You are a part of me.

We are ONE.

So when I say, 'I am that I am',

I am you!!!

Blessings, Dear Hearts.

(18th March 2013)

16

EACH BEING ON THE EARTH PLANET IS RESPONSIBLE FOR THE ENERGIES THEY RADIATE FORTH

(The Circle opens with the Sounds of the Tibetan bowls and the drum)

Allow yourselves to relax completely, letting any tension within yourself flow away on the fading sound of the Tibetan bowls, releasing any pent up anger, any disharmony within the cells of your body, allowing them all to be embraced by the energy of Divine Love and transmuted into pure Light and pure Joy.

It is all too easy for Humans to hold the tensions and the stresses of the world within the cells of their body, and when this is allowed to happen over long periods of time, you begin to create dis-ease within your physical vessel. It is important therefore to take the time to relax, to move into your Heart and to consciously ask for the disharmonious energies within you to be released with ease and grace in a manner which transmutes them into Divine Light, so that you do not simply discard your dis-harmonious energies and allow them to flow to others.

You are always responsible for the thoughts and feelings within yourself, and when these are dis-harmonious you have the responsibility to transmute those thoughts and feelings, to cleanse yourself and cleanse the world around you. *You do this Dear Hearts by embracing Love, total unconditional Love, non-directional Love, Love as an energy, Love as a state of Being.*

Feel your physical body now, seek out any disharmonious energies, wrap them in Love and allow them to be transmuted into Light, to fill the room with Light, to fill the Earth with Light. Each Being on the Earth Planet is responsible for the energies they radiate forth, and when they accept that *'like energy attracts like energy'*, then they know what they need to create within themselves, the energies of Divine Love, Divine Light, and Divine Joy, so that these can be amplified by what they attract to themselves.

What others attract to themselves is influenced by the energies that you create and radiate. *Focus then on the Love within your Heart and see that Love becoming a brighter and brighter Love, radiating forth, embracing ALL, transmuting.*

You have been told many times, Dear Hearts, that you are co-creators of your Earth. *It is for you to decide if you wish to create a world imbued with your dis-harmony, or a world imbued with your Love.*

It is always an individual choice of what you create within yourselves, and what you radiate forth to others. Take a moment to embrace every cell of your body and create within each cell the energies you desire most, for the World you desire most.

You may feel disheartened at times when it appears that you do not create anything beyond your own physical vessel, but I am here to tell you, Dear Hearts, that each time you radiate forth the Love in your Hearts, that energy does not stop at the boundaries of your physical body, it moves outwards, seeking out 'like energies', combining with 'like energies' to empower Love throughout the Earth.

You may not always see the effects of the energies you radiate forth, but know there is an effect throughout the whole of the Earth. So *BE LOVE, FEEL LOVE, RADIATE LOVE,* and as you practice this, Dear Hearts, you will realise that more and more you are holding a Light of such intensity that no darkness can come into your Hearts again.

Do not judge yourselves on the basis of what you perceive in your outer World, do not seek to accept responsibility for those aspects of life that are not within your control, you can influence the way the World is created, but you cannot command it completely. You are a part of the whole, but you are not the 'whole'.

Focus on the contribution of energy that you bring in to the *New Earth*. Focus on Love, Focus on Joy, and more and more you will see Love and Joy around you, and *as more and more Illumined Ones upon the Earth project and radiate the Love and the Joy, the more the Earth itself BECOMES those energies.*

Dear Hearts, I am The Germain - The I am that I am, and I thank you for sharing your Love, and your Light with me tonight.

(17ᵗʰ February 2014)

17

FEEL THE POWER OF THE OCEANS FLOWING THROUGH YOUR ENERGY FIELD

(The Circle opens with the Sounds of the Tibetan Bowls and the Blessings Chimes)

Allow yourselves to relax, and move inside your Heart Chakra and embrace the Light that is your true Being. All too often you look outwards, and not inwards, but at this particular time of great change it is important to look inward, to honour that which is within you. *Honouring the Divine Being that is within you is not Ego, it is DIVINE.* For in acknowledging the Divine Light within yourself you allow yourself to honour the Divine Light within others. It no longer becomes a competition between Beings, it becomes an acceptance of all Beings. You do not need to honour others only if they are the same as yourself, you need to honour others for who they are, and to honour yourself for who you are. *Acceptance of difference is an acceptance of the Oneness of all that is.*

Greetings Beloveds, I am the Germain, the I am that I am, and I come here tonight to embrace you all with the Divine Love within my Heart, and to acknowledge and applaud the sustained work that all of you have done over many aeons of time to bring this Planet to its current state of ascension. There have been times I know that you have felt this would never happen, and even now it is easy to think that it is an illusion, but I can assure you, Dear Ones, this is the Real Deal. The shift of the Earth into its new Dimensional frequency has already taken place, and some of you here present are engaged on a daily basis in sustaining this change of vibrational frequency, you are literally becoming two and not one, one foot in one Dimension, and one foot in another, seeking to sustain the energies of both. Is it any wonder that at times you feel quite drained and tired. This will ease as more and more Light comes into the new Earth frequency, and more and more of the old anchors to the old frequencies are set aside.

Soon we will be joined in the Marine Meditation, and once again we will connect your Hearts and your

Consciousness to the Consciousness of the Oceans of this Planet. You will feel the up swell of Divine Love that will flow back into your Hearts from the Oceans of the World, for their Consciousness also has been working for aeons of time to allow, to commit, to ensure that this day comes when the Earth shifts its frequencies and takes its rightful place in the Cosmos of Light.

I would like to take this opportunity to thank each and every one of you for working with the Oceans of this place. I said many years ago that Humans have forgotten the importance of the Oceans to the wellbeing of the Earth Planet. All of you have helped to promote the idea, the concept, that the Oceans are Conscious Beings of Light that the creatures within the Oceans are Conscious Beings of Light, that you are all part of the **ONENESS**, part of a Divine collection of Beings in many shapes and forms that have come together at this time to elevate the Earth into the Light.

I thank you, each and every one of you, for the work that you have done, and no doubt the work you will continue to do, because your work with the Consciousness of the Oceans is not ending, it is beginning again on a new frequency level. More and more Light will pour into the Oceans of the Earth. The crystalline structure of the Earth will be changed, you are a part of that, for you have chosen to connect yourselves with the Great Ocean Consciousness.

Focus for a moment on the Heart beat of this Planet, the Heart beat of the Oceans, connect yourself through the Divine Light in your Heart with Beloved Whale, Beloved Dolphin, Beloved Dugong and Beloved Turtle. They are but four of the creatures of your Oceans as Humanity has perceived them, but we perceive them as Beings of Light and great Wisdom, speaking to you Heart to Heart. Feel their presence within you, open your Love to them.

As we come together again at the Equinox we will participate in a ceremony of great significance, one that will have a dramatic change effect on the Earth Planet. The energies of Peace have finally taken root within the Earth, and within the Oceans, and it is this energy of Peace that will create the greatest changes Humanity has ever seen.

Hilarion has already spoken to you through the message this one has read, and Beloved Djwahl Khul also adds his Light and his Love to the gathering

David J Adams

here tonight, we welcome them and we look forward
to sharing this special time with you at the Equinox.
It has indeed been a great honour for me to be a part
of this, and to feel your Light and your Love in my
existence. Once again I thank you all for sharing
your Light with me.

Feel the power of the Oceans flowing through your
energy field, feel the upliftment of Light, feel the
Balance and Harmony, but most of all, feel the
energy of *PEACE* radiating through every aspect of
your Being in all Dimensions, **I am the Germain,
the I am that I am, and I bless you.**

(15th March 2010)

18

YOU WILL BOTH FIND - AND CREATE - MIRACLES IN YOUR LIFE

(The Circle opens with the Sounds of the Tibetan Bowls, the Blessings Chimes and the Drum)

Greetings, Dear Hearts, I am the Germain, the I am that I am

Focus your attention on the area between your Heart and your throat - the area known as the Thymus, the High Spiritual Heart - direct connection to your Higher Self. Open and activate your High Heart Chakra, to the illumination of the energies flowing to the Earth at this time.

You are moving your perceptions of life into Higher Dimensional Frequencies, allowing you to see more, to understand more, to embrace more of yourself, of your own journey upon the Earth.

You will begin to see your own journey in its entirety, instead of in its individual components of what you call "life times on the Earth".

This is not about familiarising yourselves with past lives. It is about understanding that you are on a continuous journey of growth, and you move through different portions of that journey in different lifetimes, but always your Soul, your Higher Self is aware of all that is taking place.

As you shift the energies upwards to the Heart Chakra, and the Higher Heart Chakra, your understanding of the totality of your journey will become clearer and clearer.

The energies of the 11.11.11 were the energies of understanding, for as it was indicated to you before, understanding is imperative at this time, to enable your wisdom to become the true enlightenment and illumination of your journey.

We would like to take this opportunity to thank each and every one of you here in this room, and all across the Earth who opened themselves on the 11.11.11, to draw into the Earth these energies of understanding - understanding on an individual basis, but also understanding on a collective basis.

As you sit within your High Heart and view the totality of your journey, you begin to understand your connectedness with all things, with all other Humans, with the Earth itself, with the myriad of Dimensions upon and within the Earth Planet.

You are moving quickly towards your Illumination, shifting your focus to your Heart and your High Heart. Your Thymus will prepare the way for your steps through the Portal of Illumination that is to come.

The energies that flowed to the Earth at the time of the 11.11.11 have been absorbed through the Light Workers, the Crystal Children, the Rainbow Children, all the New Souls upon this Earth, and they will radiate forth and manifest within the physical of your Planet, in changes which will become increasingly visible to all upon your Planet.

A time of great Transition, and in times of Transition there will be sorrow and sadness, and joy. It is all about perceptions and perspectives.

It is time to move your perceptions upwards into the Higher Dimensional Frequencies of your High Heart, to open your connectedness to your own Soul guidance.

Each of you has been changed by your experience on the 11.11.11, even though this might not yet have manifested itself within the physical realms of your life, but this will happen, and you will be aware when it does, and you will understand the changes that are taking place for you and for the collective of Humanity.

Be balanced in love.

Be grounded within your own Heart, and

You will both find - and create - miracles in your life.

Our thanks and our Blessings go with you tonight.

And so it is.

(14th November 2011)

19

YOU HAVE CHANGED YOUR EARTH INTO SOMETHING OF IMMENSE BEAUTY, IMMENSE POWER

(Tibetan Bowls Sounded)

Aahhh Beloveds. If you could but see the Light that is radiating forth from the Earth at this time, you would be in awe, as we are in awe.

Greetings, Dear Hearts, I am the Germain – The I am that I am.

The transformation of the Crystalline Grid System of the Earth has been profound. The absorption of Cosmic Light and the refraction of Cosmic Light has been intense and immense.

We are in awe of what you have achieved, beyond anything that we dreamed possible. So much so, Dear Ones, that we have all needed to come together in conclave to work out what we will be able to do next to assist the Earth. For within your Transformation of the Equinox, you have leapt forward to a much greater degree that was ever previously contemplated.

You should feel proud of what you have done, and not be fearful of what is to come. You have bypassed scenarios. It has never been our role as Ascended Masters to give prophesies of the future. We have only ever given you possibilities - because we have accepted and acknowledged that you, as co-creators, were solely responsible for the direction that you, and your Planet would take.

In your terminology of the day, you could say it is a little like *"computer modelling"*. Computer modelling takes the facts of the now, and then projects forwards various scenarios that are possible if certain things materialise.

This is how it has been for us and for you. We look at what you have achieved to this point in time, and we project forward possibilities of how this will eventuate if certain things then happen.

You understand what I am saying Dear Ones? Computer modelling – this is psychic modelling, cosmic modelling, but never in our wildest dreams did we perceive the changes that would take place at the Equinox.

You have literally thrown out your old computer modelling, for you have changed your Earth into something of immense beauty, immense power, and we all have to start again in looking towards what is possible for the future.

We have all been gathered in conclave, looking at the new scenarios, looking at the possibilities, looking at the potentials of the Earth, and we are in awe of what is to be.

Over time, as the energies of the Earth settle again into this new amazing Light Frequency, computer modelling will again take place, and perhaps we will not underestimate the Light within your Hearts to the degree that we did before.

Many, many more Light Beings are awakening on your Planet. The Earth itself has been changed totally. The Earth too will take time to settle and adjust to the new Light Frequencies within the Unified

Crystalline Grid System, but this will not result in the traumas that many forecast, for the Earth has absorbed these energies in a most amazing way. The Earth too is on the threshold of new and even more beautiful scenarios.

So I come tonight to applaud all of you, not merely those here within this circle tonight, but all of you throughout the Earth that have opened their hearts and poured their Love into the Earth, into the Oceans, into the Crystalline Grid Systems of your Planet.

I am sure many of you have noticed the flow of powerful energies since the time of the Equinox. Those who have been sensitive to these energies in the past, may even have been "put out of whack", you might say, by the pure force of these energies.

As I say, you do not fear them, Dear Ones. Love these energies for they are *your* creations, and you have moved the Earth, moved it to a new frequency pattern of Love and Light.

There is to be a short period of acclimatisation to these new energies, before a new surge of Cosmic energy flows through your Earth at the time of the

11.11.11. *Hang on to your seat belts, Dear Ones. You are in for another surge of energy like nothing you have ever received before,* for the absorption of the energy by the Earth has been increased The absorption of energies within you has been increased. Everything is now at a much higher level, a much higher frequency, for *you are moving now from the Transformation to the Enlightenment.*

Powerful. Powerful times. I ask you all to remain within your open Heart, and beam your Light across the Earth to awaken even more of the Light Beings that are here to assist the Earth at this time, that have not yet awakened themselves.

Allow these words to sit with you for awhile.

These are monumental times of change.

Embrace them all.

Embrace our Love as we embrace yours.

Sound your Love to the Unified Crystalline Grids of the Earth.

And so mote it be.

(10th October 2011)

20

THE TIME OF ENLIGHTENMENT IS FILLING THE EARTH PLANET

(The Circle opens with Sound of the Blessings Chimes, the Tibetan Bowls and the Drum)

Infuse every aspect of your Being with the myriad of Light frequencies radiating forth from the centre of your Circle, embrace each and every colour frequency, each and every colour movement, and feel it translating within you into energies of upliftment, energies of Joy - and let your eyes be bathed by every colour frequency, that you may look out upon your World through the eyes of Joy. For if you see your World through the lens of Joy you will assist the Earth Planet in uplifting itself into those Joyful energies, *for you create your reality by the perceptions within your Heart.*

Take a moment to allow these colour vibrations, these frequencies of Light to empower you, and through you to empower the whole of the Earth Planet.

Greetings, Dear Hearts, I am the Germain, The I am that I am.

You are here on the Earth Planet at this time with deep Love in your Hearts, and you have been asked to express that Love more frequently, more powerfully, so you can paint the World with your words in the multitude of colour that exists within your Hearts.

The time of darkness is passing quickly and the time of Enlightenment is filling the Earth Planet. It is filling the Earth Planet through the Hearts of all Humanity. *The way-showers are opening their Hearts and allowing these colour frequencies within their Hearts to cascade across the Planet.* Others will soon follow your example, firstly finding the Light within their Hearts and then opening their Hearts and allowing their Light to radiate forth, and you create a jigsaw of colour frequencies, embracing Mother Earth, enabling Mother Earth to grow, to

Heal, to **BE** the Planet of Love and Peace that it was always intended to be.

As we have said many times, it is not about what you do, it is about how you **BE** in your life. Take time each day to find the 'Beingness' within your Heart, and to empower that, and guide that, so that it can radiate forth freely - unencumbered by fear - bright Light, shining forth from the Love within your Heart.

Light and Sound are so important to your Planet, it is why we constantly come to you, Dear Hearts, and ask for you to share your Light, to ask for you to share your Sound, for as each new Being awakens and adds their Light and their Sound to the wholeness of the Earth, the Ascension journey speeds up, and the darkness of the past fades.

Focus on the Light within your Heart and take every opportunity to Sound forth the Love within your Heart, your Love for the Earth, your Love for the Oceans, your Love for Humanity, and your Love for all those other Beings of Light that are beyond Humanity - the seen and the unseen - for you are ALL a part of the WHOLE.

Oneness is no longer a concept, Oneness has become a reality in the Hearts of all those who have awakened, and the Oneness will grow as more and more are awakened to the Light and the Love within themselves.

Sharing your Light, sharing your Love, sharing your Sound, *All* of this is important in this time of great transition and transformation on the Earth Planet, and *we - your Spirit friends, those whom you call Masters, or Archangels - we stand with you, shining our Light equally, for we do not consider ourselves above you, we consider ourselves a part of you, one more speck of Light within your Heart, and we embrace that with deepest Love,*

FOR WE ARE ALL ONE

(9th February 2015)

21

NEW SOUL ORBIT WITHIN THE COSMOS

(The Circle opens with the Sound of the Blessings Chimes, The Tibetan Bowls and the Drums)

Breathe in the energy of Joy, feel it fill every aspect of your Being and allow yourself to rise on the wings of Joy into your Soul Dimension, that you may see more clearly the panorama of your Earthly life. That you may let go of your judgments of yourself and of others and simply acknowledge the *Blessedness of all things.*

Breathe in and be uplifted in Spirit, and as you breathe out, radiate forth the Joy from the centre of your Heart, bathing the whole of the Earth Planet with your *Resonance of Joy,* and notice immediately how the Earth begins to vibrate with the frequency of Joy. Look down upon the plants, the forests, the mountains and see them shine with the new energy of Joyfulness.

Greetings Dear Hearts, I am the Germain, the I am that I am.

You are in a powerful time of change upon the Earth, the last vestiges of the old world are crumbling around you, it is time for you to reach out and embrace all around you with the Light from your Heart, not the judgment from your mind.

There is much turbulence upon the Earth at this time, both of a physical nature and of a Human nature, but know, Dear Hearts, this is all part of the natural flow of the changes that are necessary for the Earth Planet at this time, for as the Earth itself expands its vibrational frequency into higher and higher Dimensions there will be a shaking of all things, of the surface of the Earth. and the surface of Humanity.

This is nothing to fear, Dear Hearts, indeed it is something to be embraced with great Joy and great eagerness, for you are being shown that all the work that you have done upon the Earth Planet in your many lifetimes is finally coming to fruition, there is no longer the anchor of darkness holding the Earth back on its journey.

Light, Love, Joy are filling every part of the Earth as it prepares to be rebirthed in a higher frequency of Light and Sound. The two cannot be separated, Dear Hearts, Light and Sound are of equal importance to the changes that are taking place now and will be taking place in the future, for this is not something that will happen in an instant, it is a progression, just as *You*, Dear Hearts, have progressed during this lifetime. There has been no instant awakening for any of you; it has been a gradual opening of your Consciousness and of your understanding of yourself and of all that is around you.

When you look back upon your life you will wonder how you came to be where you are now, considering where you were then and you will look around you at all those that have contributed to your journey, and you will acknowledge that not all lessons have been pleasant lessons, but none the less they have been important lessons and necessary lessons for you to achieve the current level of Consciousness and acceptance. And so it is with the Earth Planet itself, not instant change, a gradual change, *an evolution* LOVE is the KEY

of the Soul of the Earth Planet to a point where it acknowledges it is time to move into the higher frequencies of Light and to begin a new journey of Joy, a journey based on Love and filled with Peace.

Many times throughout the history of the Earth Planet there have been subtle changes and at times dramatic changes, but it is all about perception and perspective, nothing is ever entirely good or entirely bad, *it is all simply an experience,* and as you have raised your Consciousness and understanding of your own journey, so too has the Earth Planet itself, and now, Dear Hearts, you both stand on the verge of a wondrous, wondrous journey of Cosmic growth, of true acceptance of the Oneness of all that is.

You have been given some indications of events that are to occur at your Solstice, and I look forward to being with you to assist in any way that I can to ensure that both you and the Earth itself moves safely, gracefully into your *NEW SOUL ORBIT WITHIN THE COSMOS.*

All your friends - your Spiritual friends, your Cosmic friends - are gathering to be with you, to embrace you, to walk alongside of you as you allow

107

David J Adams

the Love within your Hearts to open completely and flood the Cosmos with more and more LIGHT.

So look around your Earth Planet, Dear Hearts, not with judgment but with Acceptance and with *TOTAL UNCONDITIONAL LOVE.*

(8th June 2015)

22

LISTEN TO THE VOICE
OF YOUR SOUL

(The circle opens with the Sounds of the Tibetan Bowls and the Blessings Chimes and the Drum)

As you close your eyes, see the most powerful Light imaginable. Normally when you close your eyes it is to take away the Light. Now when we close our eyes, we need to be seeing more and more of the Light that is shining from within ourselves. We are closing our eyes to the Light that is not part of ourselves, that is outside ourselves, *and we look within to the Light that is within our Hearts and our Souls.*

We embrace that Light powerfully, lovingly, accepting that what is within us is more powerful, more profound than anything we may experience from outside ourselves.

David J Adams

It is time, in this TIME OF AWAKENING

To awaken to the power within.
To find the passion within ourselves.
The passion for life upon this Earth.
The passion for the freedom of ourselves, and
The Freedom of our Souls to expand into multidimensional aspects of ourselves

This is not about isolating ourselves by going within, it is about connecting ourselves by going within, for it is the Light within ourselves that connects us to others, that connects us to the Earth, that connects us to the Cosmos. It is the Light within ourselves, and until we find and embrace and become that Light within ourselves, we are not connecting – we are separating.

This is the third Dimensional energies. We have moved beyond that. *We are experiencing the fifth Dimensional frequencies of Light within ourselves.*

Embracing our own Light enables us to embrace ALL, for the Light within ourselves is the Light of Divine Love, and Divine Love embraces ALL – and excludes nothing. FOR WE ARE ALL ONE.

So move your awareness now, deeper and deeper into yourself, finding the Light becoming brighter and brighter and brighter, until nothing is hidden from you. The shadows, the darkness of fear no longer exists within the cells of your Being. The final remnants of the third Dimensional past is transformed by the power of the Light within you. In that Light, embrace your Higher Soul, embrace its vision, embrace the beat of its Heart, and look around, and see the Earth in its new Light, in its new beauty, and feel the *LOVE*, feel the power of *JOY*, and *HARMONY*. And within that Love, Joy and Harmony is the Healing of all things – *for "dis-ease" are the shadows of another Dimension.* Transform those shadows with your Light, allow your Light to expand to encompass all around you, shining the Light on their shadows, transforming and transmuting those energies of "dis-ease" into Love, Divine unconditional Love.

Now let your imagination create within you the visions of the *DIVINE BEING that you are. See your life though the Inner Vision of Love.* See yourself vibrating to the new frequencies of Light and Love, and see the Earth begin to sparkle, begin to come alive with the new energy, an energy that you are creating with your imagination, for *your Imagination is your Soul speaking to you. Listen to the voice of your Soul.* Allow your imagination to create the life you are moving into.

111

Take a moment to simply feel the powerful vibration of this new incredible energy that is the *NEW EARTH* that you are creating with every thought, every breath – *YOU ARE CREATING!*

Allow your imagination to soar like the Eagle, to sit high above the Earth and see everything in a new Light of Love, and hear the sounds of JOY, the HARMONY OF LOVE.

Allow each beat of your Heart to pulsate out into the Earth these new vibrations of love, and *BE WHO YOU CAME HERE TO BE.*

I am the Germain – the I am that I am.

Take into yourselves the message of the Germain. – the I am that I am.

> *I am the Light.*
> *I am the Love.*
> *I am the Joy.*
> *I AM THAT I AM.*

So be it.

(7th February 2011)

23

FIND THE FAITH WITHIN 'YOU'

(The Circle opens with the Sounds of the Blessings Chimes and the Tibetan bowls)

Feel yourselves being carried upwards on the gossamer wings of Sound into your Soul Dimension, leaving behind the dross of your daily lives and embracing the totality of *All that is*, accepting the *'Now'* moment that is your Soul Dimension and within that Dimension reach out your arms and embrace the Earth with total Love.

Feel it as a powerful wind caressing the Earth Planet, knowing that you are a part of that wind, *that your Love is capable of uplifting the whole of the Earth Planet into the realms of Joy, Bliss and Ecstasy,* for in your Soul Dimension there are no shadows holding you back, there is only *PURE LIGHT.*

Greetings, Dear Hearts, I am the Germain - The I am that I am.

It is a great delight for me to be with you once again at this critical turning point of your individual and collective journey. The energies that have been drawn into the Earth Planet over the last two Equinoxes have dramatically changed the vibrational frequency of you - as well as of the Earth Planet itself.

I am sure, Dear Hearts, that each and every one of you has felt this vibrational change within yourself. For some it has been an upliftment, for others great concern that you may have lost your direction, but do not worry, Dear Hearts, for each of you will know what is ahead when you look deep into your Heart with Love, not fear.

Times of great change are always disconcerting to Humanity, so it is important to take your time, to move within yourself, to embrace yourself with *Love* and allow that Love to create your future.

You have been, over the last few days, through your Christian time of renewal, of death and rebirth, your Easter, and for each of you this *IS* a time of death and rebirth, of letting go the old and embracing the new.

It is a time of great Love, it is also a time of *'FAITH'*, and when I speak of faith, Dear Hearts, I do not refer to religious beliefs, *I refer to the faith you need to have for 'yourself', faith that through Love you WILL create your new reality.*

There is no written recipe to guide you through these changes - it is all to do with *'FAITH'*.

Faith is that inner knowing, that inner understanding that through Love everything is possible, and when you have faith within yourself you can step forward in your life knowing that you will create the right journey for you, and that journey will, of itself, allow you to gift to the journey of others and to the journey of the Earth Planet itself.

Yes, Dear Hearts, *'FAITH'* is one of those words that has been corrupted by religious beliefs. *Faith is just knowing that you are filled with Love, and Love creates ALL.*

I ask you to think about that, Dear Hearts, to set aside your pre conceived ideas of the word *'FAITH'* and apply it to yourself, not to the externals of religious belief, *apply it to yourself.* Ask yourself *'do I have faith in ME?'* - A powerful question that each and every Being needs to ask, for when you have faith in *you*, you are unstoppable, you change possibilities into probabilities, *you enlighten the world simply by being YOU and shining your Light, for it is the Light of Love within the Hearts of all Humanity that is the foundation of the Ascension of the Earth Planet and the future of mankind upon the Earth Planet.*

So, as the new energies gather throughout the Earth and throughout your own physical and emotional bodies,

Find the faith within YOU and allow your Joy to Light the World.

(6ᵗʰ April 2015)

24

JOY SIMPLY IS THE ESSENCE OF BLISS

(The Circle opens with the Sounds of the Tibetan Bowls and the Blessings Chimes)

Greetings, Dear Hearts, I am the Germain, the I am that I am.

As we close our eyes and focus on our Hearts, we embrace the Divine Essence of ourselves, and we ask that this Divine Essence radiates forth as the Light of Divine Love, sharing the Light of Love with others, allowing the Light to be a beacon for those who need a beacon in their lives, but to place upon that radiating Light, no conditions, no expectations of outcomes.

We also embrace the Divine Wisdom of others, knowing that we will create with that Wisdom the Light we radiate from ourselves.

At our last gathering, beloved **Ar'Ak** spoke of reactive and proactive. This is exactly what we are talking about now. For too long on this Planet, those with Wisdom to give have sought enslavement with this Wisdom, sought to create Adoration, sought to create outcomes in the lives of others.

It is time now to let go of this need for Adoration, of this need for preconceived outcomes for others, and simply allow the Divine Love within you to radiate forth as a Gift to Humanity - not as down payment on your expectations of others, but as a Gift freely given, a Gift of Light, a Gift of Love.

It is time for each one of us to walk the walk, to move forward within the Divine Love and Light, and simply to be what we were always intended to be – *Divine Beings of Light coming together in ONENESS, empowering the Earth, empowering ourselves, simply being the Light.*

It is imperative in this time of great change to apply discernment to all you see.

To apply non judgement to all you see.

To simply radiate your Divine Love, your Divine Light.

To create within yourselves the energies with which you meet the rest of the world.

Focus now deep within your heart. Feel the Divine Serenity of Peace that simply being the Light that you are allows you to be – ***Deep, Serene, Peace.***

Allow that Peace to flow outwards on the wings of Joy - for Joy has no judgement - Joy has no expectations - Joy simply is the essence of Bliss, from the deepest part of your Being.

Feel your Oneness with all that is.

Feel your Oneness with beloved Earth.

Feel your Oneness with all the Beings of Nature upon this Earth.

Embrace ***ALL*** with the Divine Love within your Hearts.

Let your Soul sing forth your Joy, surrounding the Earth with the vibration of your Bliss.

Remember always to proclaim:

"I am, the I am that I am"

"I am, the I am that I am"

"I am, the I am that I am"

"I am a part of all that is".

Blessings be upon every one, every thing upon this Earth.

So be it.

(4 July 2011)

25

AUTUMN IS A TIME OF REFLECTION AND EXPRESSION OF GRATITUDE

(The Circle opens with the Sounds of the Tibetan Bowls and Tingsha Bells.)

Greetings, Dear Hearts, I am the Germain, the I am that I am

Relax and empty yourself completely of all energies that are not uplifting. Allow the Sound vibrations of the Bowls to drive out the shadows within your minds and within your bodies, and simply sit a moment in the deep tranquillity of the Love within your Heart.

Feel that unconditional Love lifting you into higher and higher Dimensional frequencies, spreading a new and beautiful Light throughout your Being and out into the room, and feel yourself becoming the

Light your Heart is creating, for everything begins within your Heart.

Breathe gently, and allow the Light to flow freely through you and around you, and feel yourself becoming a part of the Oneness and Unity of the Love within this Circle.

As you feel the empowerment of the expanded Light of all within the Circle, imagine that Light flowing outwards across the Earth, through the Earth, touching and embracing all of Humanity, all of Nature, and feel yourself connecting with the Light of Love from within the Earth, and radiating that Light outwards even further into the Cosmos, connecting and embracing all that is.

Feel yourself as Oneness, and feel all the limitations you have placed upon yourself in this lifetime melt away, allowing the connection with your Higher Self and your Soul self to become more powerful, more certain, more important.

Let go of all that holds you within the limitations of the third dimension, and feel yourself dancing out into the Universe, a bright Light of Oneness.

The energies of this time are challenging all Light Workers to look within themselves, not in judgment of themselves, but in acceptance of themselves, for this is an Autumn of many Cosmic cycles.

Autumn is a time of reflection and expression of gratitude. It is a time to look at how the realities of your life have matched the dreams you began with, and to give thanks for all the experiences of your lifetime, for each and every one of them has brought you to this place, brought you to this space of Divine Love, unconditional Love.

There are those who will experience this and determine that they do not wish to move forward, for they cannot accept that the realities of now are not the dreams of then, and they will leave.

There are many, many Light Workers who will accept this time of reflection and embrace all that has been and look forward with great Joy and great Light in their Hearts, for they have come in service to the Earth, and they can see beyond the limitations of the third dimension, and view their lives from a higher perspective and come to different conclusions. They will express their gratitude and move on as shining Lights for others.

It is a time of great change for all upon the Earth, a time to let go of judgements, a time to embrace acceptance and step forward.

Feel the Love and the Light and the promise that is in the energy flowing into the Earth at this time.

Embrace it.

   Become it.

      Accept your own Divinity, and

         Accept yourself as part of ALL THAT IS.

(3rd September 2012)

26

EACH BEING OF LIGHT HAS A UNIQUE VIBRATIONAL FREQUENCY

(The Circle opens with the Sounds of the Tibetan bowls, the Blessings Chimes and the shakers.)

Focus on the stillness at the centre of your Being, and within that stillness open yourselves to all the possibilities of multidimensional existences, drawing into yourself Light Beings from all Dimensional Frequencies and from all across the Cosmos, embracing them with the Love deep within your Being and inviting them to share with you their wisdom, that they may contribute to your growing awareness of your *'ONENESS WITH ALL THAT IS'* - and invite them to speak openly and lovingly.

Greetings, Dear Hearts, I am The Germain - The I am that I am.

It is important now in this moment to feel the presence of all the Beings of Light from throughout the Universe, that you may finally accept in your Hearts that you are no longer alone, you are no longer separate and you are certainly not forgotten. All your Spiritual friends have gathered here tonight, you can sense them, you can feel them, you can hear them breathing into the Circle, breathing the energies of Love.

We do not exist within your minds, we exist within your Hearts, and the more you become aware of this and acknowledge this and accept this, the greater will be your connection and communication with all those Beings of Light who seek to be a part of your journey - not only that they may assist you, but that you may assist them, for every Being of Light, irrespective of what Dimension they are within or what part of the Cosmos they are in, are on a journey of growth, a journey that is not made in isolation and separation, but is made in the embrace of **ONENESS**.

Each Being of Light has a unique vibrational frequency - vibrational frequencies themselves hold wisdom and knowledge, and simply being within that vibrational frequency creates an exchange of wisdom and knowledge.

On Planet Earth, Dear Hearts, you are so accustomed to language that you forget there are a myriad of other ways of communicating and the essential method of communication that exists in all Dimensions and throughout the Universe is the interaction of energy frequencies, different frequencies of Light, different frequencies of Love.

Each Being you meet will involve an exchange of energy, you may not know each other's languages, but you KNOW each other's energies.

In your minds, Dear Hearts, you give lots of different names to this, telecommunications, telepathy, lots of different expressions, but what you are talking about is simply an exchange of energy and through that energy an exchange of wisdom and knowledge.

You can stand next to someone on a train or on a bus or in your shopping centre and share no words, and yet you will have interacted in your energy and you will each have gifted to the other wisdom and knowledge, and you will have grown from that interaction, and when, like tonight, you invite into your Circle all the Beings of Light from other Dimensions and other places in the Cosmos, there is an amazing exchange of wisdom that is happening.

Each of you will respond to it differently, each of you will give differently and receive differently and once you allow your mind to be set aside and to acknowledge this exchange of energy, you will begin to allow that wisdom and that knowledge to become a part of your awareness, a part of your understanding and you will begin to feel the joyfulness of connection, connection beyond your time, beyond your life spans, for they do not exist in this oneness, *this melting pot of wondrous wisdom.*

From time to time, Dear Hearts, we come to you as individuals and share perceptions and perspectives that you may not have recognised previously, but at all times we come as a *"Community of Oneness"*, both to gift and be gifted, to give and to receive, for when you open the Light of this Circle to the Cosmos it draws into its Heart those that need assistance in their journey and those who wish to gift assistance to others, to you, to others in different Dimensions, to others within the Cosmos, you are all one and you are all together here tonight.

Let your minds be still, let your Hearts be open and active, and let yourselves absorb the wisdom of ALL THAT IS, and feel the joy, feel the gratitude, feel the magic of ONENESS at work.

You may choose to speak to some but not to others, that is a personal choice, you will be drawn to those from other places that resonate with your energies, that need to receive from you your Love, or need to give to you their Love.

It is not a place of judgment, it is a place of sharing, it is the Heart - the Heart of Pendragon - and it is open to all those of the Light, to all those who need the Light.

Dear hearts, we so enjoy sharing with you, being with you, and we embrace you with deepest, deepest Love.

(1ˢᵗ February 2016)

GLOSSARY

Ascended Masters - Spiritually Enlightened Beings who have previously incarnated in Human form on the Earth but who are now in Higher Dimensional Frequencies.

Wesak – A celebration of the Birth, Enlightenment and Ascension of the Buddha.

Shambhala - A 'City of Light' in Higher Dimensional frequencies where Spiritual and Cosmic Beings work together in Oneness. Some perceive it to be situated Energetically above the Wesak Valley in Tibet. Channeled information given to me indicates that Shambhala is a structure within the Etheric comprised of 6 energy Pyramids of the 4 sided variety, connected together to form the Sacred Geometric shape of a Merkaba.

Pendragon – When David J Adams moved house in 2006 he was told in a dream that the House would be called 'Pendragon', so from that time his Meditation Circle became known as Pendragon Meditation Circle. Pendragon, of course, was the Name given to Welsh Kings of old like Uther Pendragon (father of Arthur of the Round Table), so could be a reflection of David's Welsh heritage.

Songlines – there are 12 major songlines throughout the Earth which come together at two places, Sundown Hill just outside Broken Hill in Australia (they are represented here by Sculptures) and Machu Picchu in Peru. They are vibrational, or Sound Arteries of the Planet. See additional information on approximate routes of each Songline on next page.

Blessings Chimes – A hand held instrument created from wind Chimes which are used to Bless the Earth, the Oceans and all Beings of Light upon the Earth.

Crystalline Grid – A structured network of Crystals throughout the Earth that are part of the electromagnetic composition of the Earth.

Equinox - An **equinox** is commonly regarded as the moment when the plane of Earth's equator passes through the center of the Sun's disk, which occurs twice each year, around 20 March and 23 September. In other words, it is the point in which the center of the visible sun is directly over the equator.

Solstice - A **solstice** is an event occurring when the Sun appears to reach its most northerly or southerly excursion relative to the celestial equator on the celestial sphere. Two solstices occur annually, on about 21 June and 21 December. The seasons of the year are directly connected to both the solstices and the equinoxes.

Marine Meditation – This was a Global Meditation initiated by Beloved Germain to be held at 8pm on each Equinox, wherever people were in the world. It focused on connecting with the **CONSCIOUSNESS OF THE OCEANS**. It ran from March 1991 to September 2012 - 22 years and 44 meditations in all. See http://www.dolphinempowerment.com/MarineMeditation.htm

Labyrinth - A Sacred Geometric Design or Pattern that creates a Path or journey to the center, and a return along the same route. On a Spiritual level it represents a metaphor for the journey to the centre of your deepest self, and back out into the world with a broadened understanding of who you are. With a Labyrinth there is only one choice to make, that choice is to enter or not, that choice is to walk the Spiritual path in front of you, or not. The choice is always yours to make within your Heart. There is no right or wrong way to walk a Labyrinth, you only have to enter and follow the path to the Center – the Center of yourself. Walk it in **LOVE**, walk it in **PEACE** and walk it in **RESPECT**.

Marine Meditation Tapestry: This is the image on the Front cover and represents all 8 Labyrinths that were walked during Marine Meditation ceremonies from the March Equinox of 2003 until the September Equinox of 2012. Each Labyrinth contained a special "Harmonic Note". From left to right the Labyrinths are –

Trinity Labyrinth of Purification, (2003) Harmonic note of "The Harmonics" - Cosmic Beings of Light that hold the Earth Planet in Balance.

Octagonal Labyrinth of Manifestation, (2004) Harmonic note of Unicorn.

Diamond Labyrinth of Transcendence, (2005) Harmonic note of Whale.

Eight Pointed Star Spiral Labyrinth of Creation (2006) Harmonic note of Dragon.

Cosmic Tree of Life Labyrinth, (2007) Harmonic note of Zadkiel and the Angelic Realms.

"Motherland of MU" Labyrinth, (2008) Harmonic note of 'The MUSE'

Labyrinth of Divine Peace, (2009 and 2010) Harmonic note of Dugong (sometimes referred to as Manatee).

Labyrinth of Inner Vision, (2011 and 2012) Harmonic note of Eagle.

LOVE is the KEY – (Book Title) This is the title of a song written, performed and recorded by David J Adams, and can be heard – and downloaded free of charge – at https://soundcloud.com/david-j-adams/love-is-the-key

SONGLINES – NAMES AND APPROXIMATE ROUTES

We have given names to the 12 Songlines that embrace the Earth Planet based on the names of the 12 Sculpture on Sundown Hill, just outside Broken Hill in New South Wales, Australia. Below we give the approximate routes that the Songlines take between Sundown Hill and Machu Picchu as they were given to us in meditation.

RAINBOW SERPENT: Sundown Hill – Willow Springs – Mount Gee (Arkaroola) – Kings Canyon (near Uluru) – Mount Kailash (Tibet) – Russia – North Pole – via the North American Spine to Machu Picchu.

MOTHERHOOD: Sundown Hill – India – South Africa – follows the Nile River to North Africa – Machu Picchu.

THE BRIDE: Sundown Hill – Pacific Rim of Fire – Machu Picchu.

MOON GODDESS: Sundown Hill – Across the Nullabor to Perth – Madagascar – Mount Kilimanjaro – Egypt (Hathor Temple) – Via the Mary Line to the United Kingdom – Machu Picchu.

BAJA EL SOL JAGUAR (UNDER THE JAGUAR SUN): Sundown Hill – Grose Valley (New South Wales) – New Zealand – Chile – Via the Spine of South America (Andes) – Machu Picchu.

ANGELS OF SUN AND MOON: Sundown Hill – Willow Springs - Curramulka (Yorke Peninsular of South Australia) – Edithburgh (also Yorke Peninsular of South Australia) - Kangaroo Island – Mount Gambier - Tasmania – South Pole - Machu Picchu.

A PRESENT TO FRED HOLLOWS IN THE AFTERLIFE: Sundown Hill – Arltunga (Central Australia) – Through the Gold Light Crystal to Brazil – along the Amazon to Machu Picchu.

TIWI TOTEMS: Sundown Hill – South Sea Islands – Hawaii – Mount Shasta (USA) – Lake Moraine (Canada) – via Eastern Seaboard of USA to Machu Picchu.

HORSE: Sundown Hill – Philippines – China – Mongolia – Tibet – Europe – France – Machu Picchu.

FACING THE NIGHT AND DAY: Sundown Hill – Queensland (Australia) – New Guinea – Japan – North Russia to Finland – Sweden – Norway – Iceland – Tip of Greenland – Machu Picchu.

HABITAT: Sundown Hill via Inner Earth to Machu Picchu.

THOMASINA (JILARRUWI – THE IBIS): Tension Lynch pin between Sundown Hill and Machu Picchu.

HOW TO MAKE YOUR OWN
BLESSINGS CHIMES

Blessings Chimes have a triangular wooden top. Inserted into the underside of the wooden triangle are a series of Screw Eyes with a series of chimes dangling from them with THREE 'Strikers' of your own design. The chimes are of different sizes, thicknesses or metals to provide a variety of Tones (which we created by taking apart a number of different, inexpensive, wind chimes). The Screw Eyes are set out in 5 rows from which the Chimes are hung, a single chime at the tip of the triangle, then 2 chimes, then 3 chimes, then 5 chimes and finally 7 chimes. This makes 18 chimes in all. One Screw Eye from which a 'Striker' hangs is placed between rows 2 and 3, and then two Screw Eyes from which 'Strikers' hang are placed between rows 4 and 5.

The 'Strikers' used in creating our Original Blessings Chime for the Marine Meditation had as decorations a Sea horse, a Unicorn, and a Dragon. The Triangular wooden top has a small knob on it, to hold as you shake the Blessings Chimes to create the vibration and resonance.

Although the original has a triangular Top and 18 chimes, you can vary this to your own intuition. The latest version that has been created for David has an Octagonal top and only 8 chimes and is called 'Peace and Harmony Chimes' rather than 'Blessings Chimes' to reflect it's more subtle Sound. Use your imagination and Intuition.

Blessings of Love and Peace

David J Adams

Printed in the United States
By Bookmasters